The Three Gates of Enlightenment

Awakening to the Original Spiritual Culture of Humanity

With 9-Week Workshop Book

Title:
The Three Gates of Enlightenment;
Awakening to the Original Spiritual Culture of Humanity
First Edition

The Three Gates of Enlightenment

Awakening to the Original Spiritual Culture of Humanity

Ahn Gyeong-jeon
His Holiness the Jongdosanim

With 9-Week Workshop Book

The Ultimate great One Mind

Dragon & Phoenix Publishing

Contents

His Holiness the Jongdosanim's lecture at Times Center in October 2016.

The Three Gates of Enlightenment:

Awakening to the Original Spiritual Culture of Humanity.

By Ahn Gyeong-jeon, His Holiness the Jongdosanim

Translator's note

In October of 2016, His Holiness the Jongdosanim gave a discourse on enlightenment at the Times Center of New York City where he presented a vision for the world to cure our ills, to heal each other, and to open up an enlightened world of brilliant radiance. That lecture is the basis of this book, which is the first book in English that he is sharing with the world. In reading this book, it will become very clear to you that His Holiness the Jongdosanim is awakened to the life of the Universe and is awakening us to be one with the life of the Universe.

His Holiness the Jongdosanim established the Jeung San Do movement in 1974. In 1977 he experienced the great spirituality of the renewal of Heaven, Earth, and Humanity. He authored numerous books during the tumultuous times of the 1980s, including *The Truth of Jeung San Do (1981)* and *This is GaeByeok (1982)*. Through his writings and teachings, he presented a vision to the youth of Korea for the way to lead a life of mutual life-bettering and life-saving. Now that those youths have grown up and are leading the nation, his teachings serve as the mantras that guide politics and economics in Korea.

In 1992, Jongdosanim first published *The Jeung San Do DoJeon*. With this book he awakened Korea to the spirituality that was lost during Japanese colonial times. In this way he was able to finally restore the lost identity of the Korean people. The Korean songs and dramas that are sweeping the world today owe much debt to His Holiness the Jongdosanim for restoring the lost Korean identity.

During the early 2000s, Jongdosanim founded the SangSaeng Research Institute and the STB Broadcasting Company to present the vision of mutual life-bettering and life-saving to the world. In 2010 he published his translation of *Hwandangogi*, a book about the ancient history of Korea that the Japanese attempted to destroy during the colonial era. During that time the Japanese rewrote Korean history to justify their occupation. They burned more than 200,000 volumes of Korean history books and then rewrote the history of Korea with the message that Korea began as a colony of China and Japan. With the publication of *Hwandangogi,* the lost history was revealed to the world and Korea was finally restored in its rightful place in history.

Since 2010, Jongdosanim has been traveling the world giving lectures on the lost spiritual and meditation teachings of Korea. Today he runs Jeung San Do centers around the world. These centers teach meditation and ways of life that heal people and the world.

About 20 years ago I had an opportunity to visit Korea and conduct meditation study at Jongdosanim's home in the city of Taejon with about 20 other students. It was an incredibly hot and humid August night.

I arrived by plane and on that very night I went to his home to participate in an all-night meditation, sitting in the yard at his house. I can remember that I was still wearing the same suit that I wore on the plane and I was sweating profusely. All I could think all night long was, "When the morning comes, I am going to go over to the Renaissance Hotel to take a long bath at the famous spa." His house was located in a city known for its natural hot spa, and I had been to that spa on a previous visit. Finally, the morning arrived, and our meditation came to an end. Jongdosanim spoke briefly and encouraged us to continue with our meditation study. Then out of the blue he said, "By the way, the spa at the Renaissance Hotel is closed for renovation."

I did not get to go to my favorite spa that day but I did become determined to pursue meditation study in earnest. In meditation study it is immensely important to fix the mind on pursuing meditation until you gain an understanding. I decided then to devote myself for the next seven days. So for seven days I stayed up all night chanting the Taeeulju Mantra in the yards of Jongdosanim's house under his guidance.

On the seventh night I saw a radiance bursting out from the direction of Jongdosanim. I felt my crown chakra open up and saw the radiance of the full moon open up in front of my closed eyes. Then, all of a sudden, the energy of the Taeeulju Mantra poured down into my crown chakra as if I was under a waterfall. I found myself skewered with the energy of the Taeeulju Mantra as if I was a shish kebab. I was stuck to the ground with that piercing energy all night. The radiance of the Taeeulju poured down into me. Even today when I sit to meditate my crown chakra opens. When it does, it feels like a cool breeze passing through me at the top of my head. It feels

like I have a top knot.

The pages of this book, filled with the words and teachings of Jongdosanim, will introduce readers to the experience of the healing radiance and magic of Taeeulju meditation.

I introduce to you, Jongdosanim! I ask you to please welcome his teachings with great appreciation.

Jaenam Kim

The Holiest Mantra Taeeulju

Introduction

I'm extremely pleased to have the opportunity to reveal the origin of the ancient spiritual culture of the East to Western society. This book that you are now reading is the first book in English to introduce these ancient teachings, which date back to more than 6,000 years ago.

In Korean Buddhist temples you always walk through three gates before you enter the main hall. Similarly, I have structured this teaching according to the three gates of knowledge that we need to pass through in order to properly understand the essence of enlightenment from the East. The first gate is the knowledge of the connection between humanity and the seven heavenly stars, a teaching that was known long ago in ancient cultures across the world. The second gate is the teaching of the pole star and the ancient numerology that is the basis of the I Ching and the concepts of yin and yang. The third gate is the culmination of these ancient, mystical

The First gate of Enlightenment at a Korean Buddhist temple. It is called "Iljumoon." It is the gate that separates the worldly realm of our living to the land of enlightenment. 1

The Second gate of Enlightenment at a Korean Buddhist temple. It is called "Chunwongmoon." It is the gate that hosts four guardian spirits of heaven who guard the land of enlightenment.

The third gate of Enlightenment at a Korean Buddhist Temple. It is called "Buleemoon," or sometimes referred to as the final gate of enlightenment. It is the entrance to the holiest place on earth. 3

Mugok(Bo)

Pagun (Pyo)

Yeomjeong (Hwa)

Mungok (Haeng)

Tamrang (Goe)

Nokjon(Gwan)

Geomun (jak)

The nine stars of the Norther Dipper

Cheonbugyeong

天符經

The Scripture of Heavenly Code

태을주 Taeeul ju

哞哆
哞哆　太乙天　上元君　哞哩哆哪都来　哞哩喊哩娑婆訶

Hoom–chi Hoom–chi Tae–eul–cheon Sang–won–gun
Hoom–ri–chi–ya–do–rae Hoom–ri–ham–ri–sa–pa–ha
훔치 훔치 태을천 상원군 훔리치야도래 훔리함리사파하

teachings, the Taeeulju Mantra, which is the the holiest mantra.

Around the world today, the practice of meditation has garnered much popularity but few people have any real knowledge about the origins of meditation culture. The message of the Taeeulju Mantra is older than even the Buddha and Confucius. The mantra contains within it the philosophy, the practice, and the experience of the original spiritual culture of the East.

It is appropriate that this book is introduced to the West through America. Both Korea and the United States of America represent the fundamental nature of the two directions, East and West. When we look at the eight trigrams of Correct Change, the United States is represented by the trigram of *tae*, known as the flower (lake). When we take a look at the United States, indeed it is a flower. It represents the diversity of the world, diversity of culture, and diversity of people.

When we take a look at Korea, represented here as the direction of the East, it is symbolized by the trigram of *gan*, which is the fruit (mountain). This represents the essence of the Eastern spiritual culture. So, when we unite the trigrams of *gan* and *tae*, (간 and 태), just as fruits come from flowers, that is really the beginning, the birth of the new age when material diversity comes together with spirituality.

Korea and the United States go beyond the relationship and bonds that we know presently in the political arena. They are bound

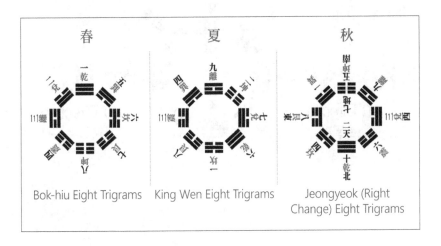

Bok-hiu Eight Trigrams | King Wen Eight Trigrams | Jeongyeok (Right Change) Eight Trigrams

by the mission of being the representations of spirituality and the diversity of humanity today. With that viewpoint, I hope you will look at Korea with love and affection.

I believe that this book will have a profound significance in the history of humanity. We have all forgotten the original culture that gave rise to human society. This original culture is the most precious thing, the greatest treasure, but we have lost it. The culture I am speaking of is the ancient Baedal nation, known today as the Hongshan culture, which once spread throughout much of present day China and Korea.

The history and spirituality of ancient Korea have been destroyed quite thoroughly in the past 100 years, largely as a result of the Japanese colonial era. During that time, the Japanese rewrote Korean history to reflect that it started as a colony of Japan and China about 2000 years ago, which is not the case. The modern world only came to know Korea as an independent country after WWII. Even then, it was really the 1950s when they came to meet Korea, during the Korean war. Unfortunately, this false version of history is still being taught around the world.

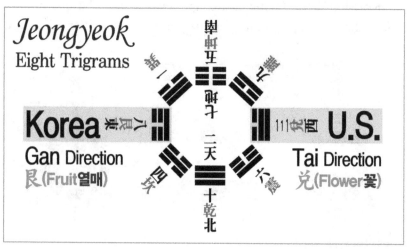

The Jeongyeok Eight Trigrams;
U.S. - Tae Direction (Flower), Korea - Gan Direction (Fruit)

In the pre-modern world, however, the Korean culture had a profound impact around the world. For example, in Persia, a great epic song, the *Kushnameh*, was written there 1,500 years ago that declared that Korea was a Paradise on earth. These songs are still performed in Iran! After the fall of Persia, some estimates claim that significant percentage of Persian population emigrated to ancient Korea. So, there was once a deep connection between the Western cultures and Eastern culture of Korea in ancient times that has been lost to today's world.

To preserve the true history of ancient Korea, I have put my best efforts into translating the *Hwandangogi*, which details the ancient history of Korea. The Japanese destroyed this book along with over

A remarkable finding that Persia and Shilla held a blood alliance.

Same daggers are found from Kazakhstan to the cave in central Asia to Korea.

200,000 others during their occupation. Fortunately, the book was preserved by the Independence Movement fighters of Korea in Manchuria.

For the past 40 years, I worked tirelessly to translate this book into Korean from the original ancient Korean, written in characters. I also had the opportunity to visit many cultural and archaeological sites mentioned in the *Hwandangogi*, from Manchuria to Eastern Europe, to confirm the validity of the book. There are common shared history, culture, and language from the Korean peninsula to Turkey and this book shows how and why.

In this book you will find many pictures of artifacts, temples, and archeological findings that serve to break any misconceptions regarding the origins of Korean culture and the roots of the practice of meditation.

This book in your hands is a brief introduction to some of the concepts of the *Hwandangogi*. In it, I share some of the things I have investigated when visiting these cultural sites and translating the *Hwandangogi*. To compile the teachings in this book I stayed up many nights over the years contemplating and meditating. I hope to convey the joyful message of enlightenment and self-healing based on my life experiences as a seeker. The message that I share is a great, hopeful message to humanity of the coming new civilization.

13 An Ham Ro, the author of the First book of Samseonggi of Hwandangogi.

三聖紀全 下篇
元董仲 撰

人類之祖曰那般與阿曼相遇之處曰阿耳斯庀蒙得
天神之敎而自成晉禮則九桓之族皆其後也
昔有桓國家言旦庶焉初桓仁居于天山得道長生舉身
無病代天宣化使人皆作力自無飢寒傳赫胥桓
仁古是利桓仁朱于襄桓仁釋提壬桓仁卻乙利桓仁至
智爲利桓仁或曰檀仁
古記云汝奈留之山下有桓仁氏之國天海以東之地亦
補汝奈留之國其地廣南北五萬里東西二萬餘里揔言

Won, Cheon-Seok (1330 -) and his Second book of Samseonggi of Hwandangogi. He was a nobleman of the court of the Koryo Dynasty of Korea. And he was also Lee, Bang-won's teacher. (Lee, Bang-won and his father founded the Joseon Dynasty of Korea.) His penname was Dong-joong. Won, Cheon-Seok is Won, Dong-joong. By compiling Second book of Samseonggi he passed down to us the lineage of the Korean civilization.

During the time of King Gongmin of Koryo Dynasty, he served as the prime minister and established a lineage of Korean history based on Shin-gyo, the spirit teaching of Korea.

Family Cemetary of Beom Family of the Geum-seong region located in Duklim-dong, Gwangju. "Bok-ae" Beom, Jang (? ~ 1395) Author of Buk-bu-yeo-gi (Chornicles of the Northern Buyeo) of Hwandangogi. He restored the lost history of Northern Buyeo.

The grave of Yi, Maek located at Yeonseo-county, Sejong-city. "IL-Sib-Dang" Yi-Maek (1455-1528) was the fourth generation descendant of "Haeng-chon" Yi, Am, who authored Dan-gun-se-gi (Chronicles of Danguns) of Hwandangogi.

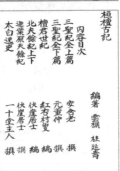

Mr. Lee, Yu-rib and his copy of the book, Hwandangogi
(picture of page 78 of the Hwandangogi book is pictured here).

Hwandangogi (*above*) reveals the primordial
culture and history of mankind

Chapter *1* The Origin of Meditation: The Hongshan Culture

It is generally believed that the practice of meditation began in ancient India, some 3,500 years ago. No one imagines that meditation might have originated in Korean culture over 5,000 ago. One reason for this is that most people mistakenly view Korean culture as merely a subtype of the Chinese Yellow River civilization and think that Korean history is less than 2,000 years old. In fact, people typically believe that Korean history is less than 200 years old. This is due to the fact that they often think the country began when it became a colony of Japan and that prior to that it was simply a part of China. Even in Korea, while the people know that their country is at least 5,000 years old, they cannot tell you what the history is because it has been erased.

The Son's Star: Jamijaegun, Je-seong (above)
The Father's Star: Gosangokhwang, Jon-seong (below)

The ideas people have about the history of Korea are a direct result of the present-day power of China and Japan and the colonization of Korea. But ancient history tells quite a different story. In ancient times, it was the Korean culture that had prominence in the region and it is here that we find the roots of Eastern spirituality and the very first practice of meditation in the world. This is explained by the fact that modern day Koreans are descendants of the ancient Baedal nation, known to archaeologists as the Hongshan culture. This culture was distinct from ancient Chinese culture and was the true origin the spiritual culture of the East.

In 1983 something was discovered that shocked the world. This *something* was found at an archaeological dig that has been excavated for the past 100 years. The site of this dig is a place called Hongshan, which is outside of the Great Wall of China, in Manchuria. The Hongshan Culture is known to be about 5,500 years old in this particular location. However, if you go to the northern part of Manchuria, you can find even older archaeological sites of the culture. Some of these sites are at least 9,000 years old.

The first item I would like you to consider is a statue of a man, or perhaps a teenage boy, who is sitting in a meditative posture. He seems to be singing or reciting something. The second item is a statue of queen, or perhaps a goddess. As you can see, she is also clearly meditating. You can even feel her virtue and nobility simply by viewing the statue.

Remains of the Hongshan Culture in Niuheliang

These artifacts, crafted between 5,000 to 5,500 years ago, are the oldest figures that have ever been discovered of people performing meditation. This is powerful evidence that humanity's original teaching of meditation was in the lands of ancient Korea.

According to Korean history book, *Hwandangogi*, Koreans came to be 6,000 years ago when the Hwan clan (which means the

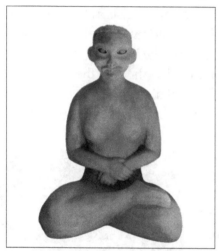

5,500 year-old pottery statue of a Goddess at the Niuheliang Yizhi Museum, Inner Mongolia, Northern China

5,300 year-old pottery statue of a God at the Aohanqi Museum, Inner Mongolia, Norther China

Goddess temple of locality 1 of Niuheliang (excavated in 1984)

brightness of the heaven, or the bright people, or the enlightened people) united with the Bear clan of the Korean peninsula and Manchuria. The story is that the Hwan clan had the population of the Bear clan go into a cave and meditate for 100 days, subsisting only by eating crown daisies and garlic. After 21 days, the people of the Bear clan were enlightened and, thus, were allowed to be united with the Hwan clan. This union became solidified when the queen of the Bear clan married the king of the Hwan clan. This is why you will find bear paws in the goddess temples of the Hongshan culture.

After seeing these statues, the next question we might ask ourselves is: what was the topic of their meditation? How were they meditating?

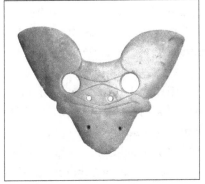

Jade Bear Head from 5,500 - 5,000 years ago. Locality 2 in Niuheliang Site, Liaoning Province Museum

Jade bear-dragon from 5,500 - 5,000 years ago, Niuheliang Archaeological Site

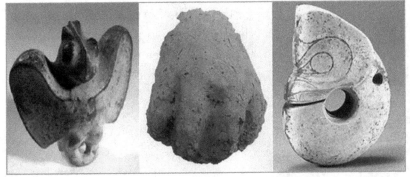

Clay stattue of a bird (left), clay figure of a bear paw (center), jade bear-dragon from Niuheliang

They must be meditating and chanting something special. What was their spiritual message? When they created these statues, what kind of message were they trying to convey? By understanding a bit more about this culture we can answer these questions.

Heaven is Round and Earth is Square

In 1983 there was another archaeological find from the Hongshan civilization that gives us insight into what the people of this ancient culture might have been meditating on: the discovery of the remains of a 150-meter structure, roughly the size of a football field. At this site, there was a square structure made of stone that was reserved for burials. Next to the burial mound was a circular altar to heaven and a goddess temple in the shape of a cross. This was discovered at location 2 at Niuheliang in Manchuria, present day North-Eastern China.

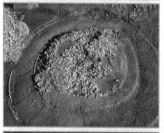

It is significant that the altar is in the shape of a circle and the tomb is in the shape of a square, as it perfectly corroborates the teachings of the ancient spiritual culture of the East that holds that "the circle is the symbol of heaven, and the square is the symbol of earth." What does it mean that Heaven is round and Earth is square? We can't afford to ignore this important message from ancient times. This is the foundation of all spiritual symbols and messages of ancient East Asia.

Excavation sites of a square shape stone mound tomb, a grand scale circular alter, and a Goddess temple which date back to 3,500 BCE was found in the Niuheliang region. This means that they had a culture that was centered around a religionous worship.

The idea illustrated here is that Heaven and Earth are the parents. Heaven is the father and Earth is the mother. The main attribute of Heaven, the great Father, is that Heaven is a harmonious mind that encompasses all things in the universe. This is represented by the geometric shape of the circle: the Round Father. The great Mother, the Earth, is represented by a Square because she is proper. In English, when we call people "square" it can have a bad connotation, but the idea is also that such people are concerned with what is proper and do not cut corners. When we have a square meal it is complete, plentiful. Mother Earth is righteous and nurtures all things. As parents, father and mother, Heaven and Earth, they produce all things on earth and in the universe.

The concept of Heaven as Father and Earth as Mother was central to the Hongshan civilization. As a result of this concept, they considered their emperor to be the son of Heaven and Earth. Cai Yong, a Chinese scholar of the Later Han period (who lived from 132-192 CE) wrote in the *Duduan, The Treatise on Ceremonial Rites*, that *Cheonja* was a title used by the *dongyi* (the ancient Chinese scholars referred to the ancient Koreans as the *dongyi*) to refer to their emperor. *Cheonja* means "son of Heaven." This later became the title used in China as well, but originally the title did not belong to the emperor of China, it belonged to the emperor of the *dongyi*, or the Koreans.

The archetype of a Heavenly Son actually comes from the Eastern culture, from the understanding that Heaven and Earth act as the parents. When we talk about the son of Heaven-- whether we're referring to the emperor of Asia or we're talking about a religious figure--the concept arises from the understanding that we are the sons and daughters of Heaven and Earth.

There are many places in the East where this concept can be seen. In the Taoist temple on the way up Taishan mountain there is a sign that reads '*Ja Gi Dong Rae*.' It was written by Lao Tzu, the founder of Taoism. The term *Ja Gi*, purple energy, originally indicated the *Jamiwon* (purple castle wall) constellation of the Northern Seven

Taishan Mountains, Shandong Provice, People's Repulic of China

'The Son of Heaven' comes from the East

Jamiwon of the Seven Stars (nine stars).

Stars. The significance of these stars will be explained in more detail later on, but the phrase refers to the energy of the Son of the God in Heaven, *Sangjenim*. *Dong Rae* means "comes from the East." So the whole phrase means, "the Son of God comes from the East," which indicates the land of Korea.

I once asked myself, "Of the hundreds of millions of people that climbed Taishan Mountain, how many of them knew the true meaning behind its ascent?" The meaning is that Korea is the land of the Heavenly King. In this sign, Lao Tzu is actually calling our attention to an ancient practice. In the past, every emperor of China would go up the Taishan Mountain and pray to the Emperor of the East, to the original emperor of Korea, because that is who gave the world the teachings of the Heavenly God.

It is important to remember that in ancient times, China was ruled from Manchuria, which was technically Korean land. Later, China gained its independence. However, the last dynasty of China before Communism, the Chung dynasty, was a Manchurian dynasty.

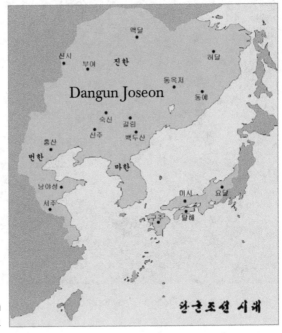

Territory of Dangun
Joseon Dynasty.

The sacred ancestor Dangun's royal portrait.

In fact, it was one of the claims of colonial Japan that they were freeing the Chinese from the Manchurians. So the only reason Manchuria is part of China today is because Manchuria conquered China, not the other way around. Even today there remains a large population of ethnic Koreans in Manchuria.

The important point, though, is that it was the emperor of Korea who originally gave the teachings of *Sangjenim*, the Heavenly Father. This is a significant point for Korean history because it shows a linguistic relationship between ancient Korea and the surrounding lands, such as Manchuria and Mongolia. These linguistic correlations even show up as far away as Mesopotamia and Eastern Europe in that they all share similar words for the Lord: *Dangun* or *Tengri*.

Dangun in Korean means 'the son of God,' or the son of Sangjenim. The son of the Hwan tribe king and the Bear tribe queen had the title of *Dangun*, as did all of the original Korean kings. The king was understood to be the manifestation of God on Earth. Therefore, the term *Dangun*, also known as *Tengri*, was being utilized around the world from central Asia to Europe. In fact, Tengrism existed in Hungary until the 10th century before the appearance of Christianity. The term Hungary even derives from Hun Gari, which

Picture of The purple castle also known as the 'Forbidden Castle' in Beijing

means the land of the Huns or Hwans. In other words, they claimed to be the descendants of the Hwan tribe. Another interesting way we can see the reach of ancient Korean culture is that Danguns assigned Khans as local chiefs so, Genghis Khan was one of the descendants of the Khans.

A further sign that this concept originates from Korea is the prominence of the color purple. According to ancient tradition, *Sangjenim* resides in a purple castle. To reflect this, the original purple castle on Earth was made for the King of Korea, which was seen as *Sangjenim's* residence. Later on, this practice was adopted by the Chinese. That is why, if you visit Beijing, the castle of the King there is called the Purple Castle. In fact, the city of Beijing itself is known as the purple city. This all traces back to ancient Korean teachings.

The idea of the Heavenly Father and Earthly Mother shows the original framework that was used to understand the nature of the self, and how the self relates to the heaven and earth. To convey this, ancient Koreans used these symbolic shapes, the circle and square. Actually, as we will see when we pass through the second gate of enlightenment, the understanding of the Heaven as father and Earth as mother was passed down from 9,000 years ago. It is based on the

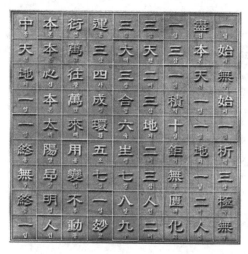

words of the Cheon-bu-gyeong (the Heavenly Code Scripture).

teachings of *Cheonbu* (the heavenly code), which derives from the *Cheonbugyeong*, the first scripture in humanity. For now, however, our main concern is simply to understand the symbolism of the burial site and sacrificial altar from the Hongshan civilization. But how is this connected to the meditating figures that were discovered to be over 5,000 years old? To understand how these are connected, we must understand a bit about the nature of meditation.

The Essence of All Meditation: Attaining One Mind

Whatever the form of meditation the ancient statues were meant to depict, we can be sure that they grasped the essence of all meditation practices that we know of today. Regardless of which tradition a particular practice of meditation is rooted in, there is one topic that is central to all meditation: arriving at one mind.

What do we mean by one mind? What does it mean when we don't have one mind? At the end of our lives, what is the difference between having one mind and not having one mind? It is, indeed, an answer that we are thirsty for. Because we all—not just Koreans, but everyone—have lost our understanding of what one mind means, and we have lost our way to find the one mind.

Today's Eastern nations of Korea, China, and Japan, as well as the rest of humanity, have completely forgotten the main theme of enlightenment that comes from the era of human genesis. We have lost the original form of our spiritual culture. It is a tragedy. Even the meditators of the East and West do not know the central topic of the original spiritual culture.

It is from the ancient remains of the circular altar to heaven and the square burial mound that we can see what the original symbolism of 'one mind' means: to attain oneness with Heaven and Earth. *This* is the answer humanity has been seeking. We must not forget that Heaven and Earth are our parents. Heaven and Earth are the great parents of all things. Therefore, we must return to a state of harmony with them. This is the basis of the one mind and the basis of all Eastern spirituality.

The idea of oneness comes from this ancient teaching which is steeped in an understanding of the different meanings that numbers have, the sacred numerology. The number *one* can refer to many things. It can refer to a unit, one unit. It can also be the beginning, the origin of everything. The name Taeeul in the Taeeul mantra actually means the ultimate beginning, the womb of the universe. This is something like the big bang point of the universe, the ultimate one. So when we say 'one mind meditation,' we are speaking of the ultimate beginning or the ultimate one. This is also represented by the one star that is fixed in the sky throughout the course of the night, the polaris. It can also refer to the unity of everything, which is the

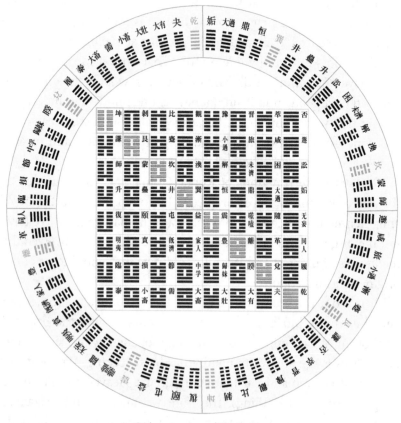

64 hexagrams of the I-ching

common meaning of oneness in meditation. When we meditate, we become one, we experience oneness. We say that all the boundaries of each person break and we become one: the border between you and I break, and we become one. However, the mantra is the thing that brings the oneness, and that occurs by returning to the origin, the womb of the universe.

The idea of one mind, the concept of being one with heaven and earth, appears in books like the *I Ching* much later in Chinese philosophy. Yet, the concept originates from ancient Korean culture, as you can see in places like Hongshan. So when we see the statues from 5,500 years ago meditating and chanting, this is what they must be chanting. They're chanting, "I want to be one with the parents, Heaven and Earth."

When we speak of chanting, we're referring to chanting a mantra, which is a code of enlightenment comprised of divine language that symbolizes the root of cosmic life. A mantra is a form of spiritual language that allows human beings to fulfill their every wish. This is why mantras are considered to be the ultimate prayer. To truly awaken and repeatedly chant a mantra with one's mind is mantra meditation.

The holiest mantra that leads humanity to the highest state of enlightenment and self-healing is the Taeeulju Mantra. But humanity has not yet properly received this holy mantra. The Mantra contains a message of hope and the essence of enlightenment in Eastern culture. It is the fruit of the enlightenment of the East, the culmination of the meditation that we see depicted in these 5,500-year-old statues. What is Taeeulju? Truly seeking out the answer to this is the essence of meditation. The answer has been hidden for many years, but I will share a very condensed explanation below and, the rest of this book will introduce and explain the meaning of the mantra more completely.

The Culmination of Meditation Practices: the Taeeulju Mantra

The Taeeulju Mantra is a healing mantra that contains the energy of every medicine and cures all diseases of the human mind and body when it is chanted with one mind. Chanting the Taeeulju Mantra allows the practitioner to become one with the universe by summoning the original ancestor of all beings in Heaven and Earth, awakening the practitioner to the creative world of the spirits.

As Taemonim, one of the original teachers of the mantra and the receiver of enlightenment from Sangjenim said, "The Taeeulju Mantra brings serenity to the mind and spirit and to the heavenly soul and the earthly soul, allowing one to experience the resplendence of the holy spirits and communion with the spirit realm. It is the mantra that will save the world's people."

The Taeeulju Mantra
Hoom-chi Hoom-chi Tae-eul-cheon Sang-won-gun
Hoom-ri-chi-ya-do-rae Hoom-ri-ham-ri-sa-pa-ha

Throughout the rest of this book I will explain the meaning behind the rest of the mantra, but first let's explore the meaning of the two sounds that begin the mantra, *hoom* and *chi*. *Hoom-chi* is the sound of calling out to the parents, Heaven and Earth. It begins with the mysterious and sacred sound *hoom*. This one character

the word Hoom

Kukai (774-835) The founder of Singong Buddhism of Japan

contains the essence of enlightenment that has been accomplished by all the previous saints, buddhas, and bodhisattvas. The ultimate source of universal life, the divinity of the Creator itself is contained in the sound, *hoom*. It is often said by the linguistic scholars that mantra is indeed the origin of letters and writing. Mantra is the origin of all sorts of human language. There is a major *bija* mantra, or seed mantra, that is used to symbolize the eternal life of the whole universe, and that is *hoom*.

The Buddhist Dictionary says, "All kinds of teachings are contained within this one character." In Buddhism, *hoom* is said to encompass "all teachings within it," the entire 84,000 sutras of Buddhism. The Japanese monk Kūkai (774-835), the founder of the Singon sect of Buddhism, said that *hoom* is the boundary of becoming one with the Three Bodies of Truth--*dharmakāya*, *sambhoghakāya*, and *nirmānakāya*. In Buddhism, it is said that the truth, the Buddha, has three bodies. The first is the body of *dharmakāya*, which is the truth, a body called *sambhoghakāya*, which is a body of gratitude, and a body of *nirmānakāya*, or transformation.

There is a difference between the *hoom* of Jeung San Do that

The three bodies of truth in Buddhism, Dharmakaya, Samhoghkaya, and Nirmanakaya

I am sharing and the *Om* in Buddhism, as in the Tibetan mantra, *Om-mani-padme-hoom*. Clearly, those two sounds are related. Some people refer to it as a rising sound and descending sound, but the best way of explaining the difference between the two is that *om* is the seed of the universe and *hoom* is the fruit. When you sound *om*, obviously it's smaller. When you say *hoom*, it's larger. So *om* is the beginning and *hoom* is the fruit that encompasses all things. *Hoom* contains everything, embraces everything in the universe.

The Indian-American doctor Deepak Chopra has also spoken of the power of *hoom*. In one of the lectures he gave based on the Quantum Healing book, he mentions that when a British scientist put cancer cells in a test tube and shot the sound *hoom* into it, the cancer cells exploded. *Hoom* is the ultimate source and the integration of all divine sounds. *Hoom* is the de facto carrier wave that contains the convergence of all sounds both sacred and holy, thereby making it the pinnacle sound in the universe thus far.

An American scholar expressed the meaning of this word by saying that the English word 'human' originally stemmed from this sound, *hoom*. Human, *hoom* man. Humanity is the manifestation of this sound *hoom*! Linguistically, I'm not sure whether this is correct or not, but isn't it a beautiful concept? When I think about it before

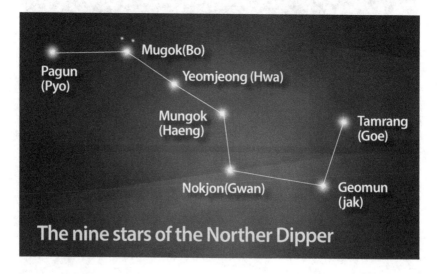

The nine stars of the Norther Dipper

sleeping and I kind of wake up, I laugh to myself. Humanity is the manifestation of the sound *hoom*.

Then, what is *chi*? The beginning of the mantra is *hoom-chi* and this is like the inside and outside of our body. *Hoom* is the inside and *chi* is the outside. When you speak the word *hoom*, you have to close the mouth and sound in, thus the sound travels inside. When you say the word *chi*, you must open your mouth and say out loud, thus expelling out all negativities. To say the word *chi* is to state and pronounce to Heaven and Earth. *Chi* means to stay in the state of eternity with the determined mind, the never-changing mind, the eternal, determined mind. It means to be one with that. *Chi* means "to establish great determination and not change". *Chi* means "to fix with determination and refrain from change." It means to become one with Heaven and Earth.

The latter half of the mantra simply re-emphasizes the first half, as if it is a refrain: *Hoom-ni-chi-ya-do-rae Hoom-ni-ham-ni-sa-pa-ha*. This is another way of saying *hoom chi* as a song of longing for wish-fulfillment and self-healing. It expresses our earnest desire and prayer, our pledge, and an expression of our gratitude for benevolence.

The other words in the mantra are *Tae-eul-cheon Sang-won-gun*, this refers to the Lord of the Seven Stars, or the Lord of the Polaris star. To properly understand this, we will need to pass through the three gates of enlightenment and go into the main story of the Taeeulju Mantra which immortals, Buddhas, Boddhisatvas and the enlightened ones have sung from heaven above, since the beginning of time. It is the song of eternal life, the song of awakening.

Chapter 2 | **The First Gate to Enlightenment:**
The Culture of the Seven Stars

To pass through the first gate of enlightenment is to gain an understanding of the cultural and historical background of the Northern Seven Stars, or the Big Dipper, and how these stars relate to the Taeeulju Mantra. This also serves to give us a deeper understanding of the meditation that the 5,500-year-old Hongshan statues were meant to convey because the culture of the Seven Stars (and the polaris, as we shall see in the following chapter) originates from this ancient culture.

In East Asia the word for civilization comes from the word for astrology. So when we speak of civilization and culture, we're talking about how advanced people are in terms of understanding of the heavens. The astrology referred to here is not focused on predictions of the future. Remember that attaining the one mind means becoming aligned with heaven and earth. It is from the stars that we can come to understand where our spirituality comes from.

What kind of stars are the Seven Stars in the Northern sky? They

The character 'Mun' is used for the word "culture," which is derived from the concept of the 'heavenly writings.'

were the foundation of the spiritual culture in both the East and the West. These stars are considered to be the origin of life. They are also thought to be the place that human beings return to when they die. The Seven Stars are therefore the land of the ancestors. They are also much more than this.

From ancient times, the Northern Seven Stars have been revered as the stars where the governor of the grand universe, God the Father, resides. The Seven Stars have been known as the Chariot of *Sangjenim*, God the Father. That was written in the book of heavenly officials, *The Shiji: The Records of the Great Historian*, a Chinese history book. The Seven Stars, therefore, have been venerated since ancient times. People worshipped the stars by offering a bowl of pure water and then bowing toward them in the northern Sky. Today the Korean people still maintain this way of worship. It is traditional to place fresh water on top of their offering given to *Sangjenim*.

It was also said that within the Seven Stars, the Governor of the Grand Universe resides in a Jade Castle and sits on a jade throne. Because of this, the Hongshan culture venerated Jade, as you can see in the many jade ornaments that have been found in that region, dating from 5,000 to 8,000 years ago. They look as if

Offering a bowl of pure water

A portrait of Sangjenim, who was born 150 years ago in Korea.

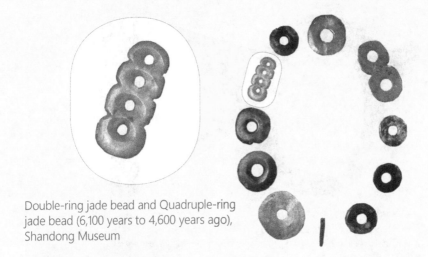

Double-ring jade bead and Quadruple-ring jade bead (6,100 years to 4,600 years ago), Shandong Museum

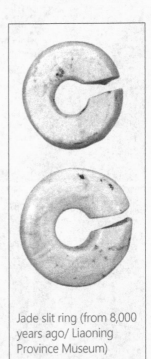

Jade gong with seventeen joints from 4,500~ 4,200 years ago. National Palace Museum, Taipei

Jade artifact with seven joints from 6,000 years ago. Chifeng Museum

Jade slit ring (from 8,000 years ago/ Liaoning Province Museum)

C-shaped jade dragon from 5,500~ 5,000 years ago. It was excavated at Wengniuteqi, Inner Mongolia Autonomous Region.

Jade artifact shaped like a person praying from 5,500~5,000 years ago. Locality 16 of Niuheliang Site, Lianoing Province Museum.

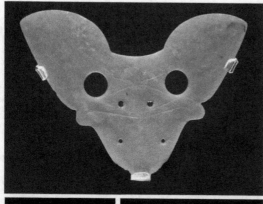

Jade bear head from 5,500~5,000 years ago. Locality 2 in Niuheliang Site, Liaonig Province Museum.

◄◄ Jade hoop for topknots from 5,500~5,000 years ago. Locality 5, Niuheliang Archaeologtical Site

◄ Jade bear dragon from 5,500~5,000 years ago, Niuheliang Archaeological Site

they were cut by lasers today, but this was all done by hand.

Originally, the Seven Stars were known as nine stars because there are two stars that exist next to the sixth star. There is a star where the Heavenly Father resides, *Go-sang-ok-hwang*, and there is also a star where the Son resides, *Ja-mi-je-goon*. These stars are also known by the names: *Jon-seong*, and *Je-song*.

The Seven Stars also correspond to the human body in a number of ways. These stars are said to shower the earth with seven different spiritual energies that comprise the physical body of a human being. Each of the stars corresponds to one of the seven chakras and fills the body with the energy associated with that chakra. The Seven Stars are also connected to the seven holes in the human face. The two other holes in the body represent the other two stars that are sometimes counted in the Big Dipper. Women, of course, have the tenth hole, which is the hole of creation, and that is represented by the polaris. Isn't this interesting? Because of the connection between the stars and our bodies, the people in the East believe that if they prayed to the Northern Seven Stars they would live a long life without illness.

The culture of the Northern Seven Stars in the East originated from the Baedal nation, or the Hongshan people, who worshipped *Sangjenim* as God the Father. Still, elements of the Seven Stars are found in Confucianism, Christianity, Judaism, Islam and Hinduism. Let us examine the prominence of this culture in Korea, China, Japan and around the world.

The Seven Stars Culture in Ancient Manchuria

In the Manchurian lands, where the ancestors of the Korean people used to live, the culture of the Big Dipper goes back at least 9,000 years. You can see the image of the great ancestor, the Grand Father, from that culture. There is one very special site honoring the Seven Stars, located in the easternmost tip of China near the Great Bear Qixing River, in the present-day province of Heilongjiang. This is known to be part of the original territory of Korea. In this place you can find an ancient castle in Fenglin. In that castle there are clearly the remains of a depiction of the Seven Stars, or the Big Dipper. The structure is thought to be 9,000 years old. Chinese authorities have cordoned off these grounds with wire fences and surveillance cameras in an effort to cover up these findings.

You can also see the culture of the Seven Stars when you look at the rituals of the people of Manchuria. If you examine the costume worn by shamans in Manchuria (who have been in existence forever) you see the Seven Stars covering the chest in the most prominent way.

At the Imperial Sacrificial Altar in Beijing, you see the Seven Star stones in the Temple of Heaven Park. The fact that the Taishan Mountain (in present day Shandong province) has seven peaks must be part of how the mountain came to be understood to have its great significance. It was understood to be a representation of the Seven Stars here on Earth.

We also find an altar to the Seven Stars in the Forbidden Palace in Beijing (also known as the Ja-Geum Palace, a name which means the Purple Palace, which refers to the Seven Stars). Next to the Heavenly Altar is a shrine created for people to offer prayers to the Seven Stars. In the yard of this shrine, you see seven stones that also represent the

Three-level altar with seven holes representing the Northern Dipper (Heilongjiang Province, China)

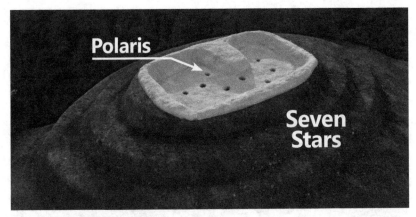

Three-level altar with seven holes representing the Northern Dipper (Heilongjiang Province, China)

seven peaks of Tianshan mountain.

Furthermore, we can see the prominence of the culture of the Northern Seven Stars in the imperial tomb of the founding emperor of the Ming dynasty, Zhu Yuanzhang. This tomb was built in the shape of the Big Dipper in 7 different locations: Hyoreung, Hamabang, Daegeummoon, Mangju, Youngsungmoon, Ohryonggyo, Hyangjeon, and Bosung.

These are just a few examples to provide an idea of how pervasive this culture was throughout 5,000 plus years of ancient Chinese history. There are many other accounts and pieces of evidence that can be examined.

The Seven Stars in Japan, Korea, and the ancient world

Throughout the ancient world, the Seven Stars culture was the basis of political life in the royal court and spiritual life in the temples. The

Manchurian Seven Stars Ceremonial Robe (Jilin Province Museum)

Seven-star Stones (Temple of Heaven, Beijing, China)

Taishan Mountains (Shandong Province, People's Republic of China)

Temple of Heaven (Beijing, China)

The Hall of Prayer for Good Harvests, at the Temple of Heaven

culture of the Northern Seven Stars was prominent in ancient Japan. In Tokyo, for example, there are seven prominent shrines that have been arranged in the shape of the Big Dipper--as you can clearly see from an aerial photograph. Also, if you look at the robe worn by Emperor Komei (1831-1867), the 121st emperor of Japan, you see the seven stars placed in prominent position, just on his shoulders.

Memorial tablet for the Big Dipper (The Imperial Vault of Heaven at the Temple of Heaven)

Another Japanese location to examine is in Tokyo, where you can visit a Japanese spirit temple built in the shape of the Northern Seven Stars. It is the Kandamyojin, the tomb and shrine of Tairano Msagado. Its structure takes on the shape of the Big Dipper. This spirit temple contains the great secret truth of the universe and the most divine mantra, the Taeeulju Mantra.

Of course, there exists a great deal of history of the Seven Stars in Korea: there are many shrines to the Seven Stars. In fact, if you go to any Buddhist temple in Korea you will find the main shrine where the Buddha is located and you will see that above the main shrine is a shrine devoted to the Seven Stars. The Seven Stars were revealed in Korea before Buddhism came in, so even though they built the temple for Buddha, they also created a shrine for the Seven Stars and kept it on a higher ground.

You can also see the remnant of the Seven Stars in architecture. In the Hwasun Unjusa Buddhist Temple they have built numerous seven-layered pagodas. This is done in many temples, but this serves as one famous example. In the picture of these pagodas, you can see that next to the seven layered pagoda, seven stones have been placed to represent the constellation of the Seven Stars.

Seven-Stars-Shaped locations of Graves and Shrines of Taira No Masakado (Tokyo, Japan)

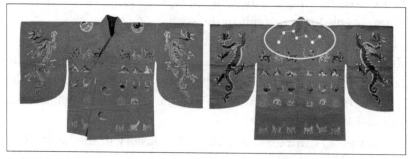

Embroidered seven stars on the Emperor Komei(1831-1867)'s Imperial Robe

In many other places, you will see the prominence of the number seven, and it refers back to the Seven Stars. For example, there is one painting where there are seven buddhas who represent the Seven Stars. In another painting they are depicted as the Seven Spirits of God. The idea is that one of these Buddhas or Gods presides over each of the stars. You can even see the culture of the Seven Stars along with the sun and the moon on the murals of the Goguryeo dynasty, which lasted from 37 BC to 668 CE.

Another place you find the Seven Stars in Korea is in coffins. When a person dies in Korea, their coffin bears the

Panoramic View of Hwasun Unjusa Temple (South Jeolla Provnice, South Korea)

Seven-Star Stones and a Seven-story stone pagoda tower (Goryeo Dynasty, Unjusa Temple, Korea)

seven holes which represent Seven Stars. The idea is that when people die they return back to the Seven Stars.

This beautiful diagram shows the truth behind the ancient Korean tradition of Spirit Teaching (Singyo). This is the Northern Seven Stars engraved on dolmens.

If we visit the royal court of the Joseon dynasty, on the ceiling there is a drawing of the sun and moon and the Seven Stars are above the king's throne.

The culture of the Seven Stars is not, however, limited to Korea, Manchuria, and Japan. Since the very beginning of time, all people of the world--including the nomadic cultures and seafaring peoples of Eurasia--found their way using the Seven Stars as their standard for direction. Whether they were on a ship or in the desert, the Seven Stars helped determine their path.

Since the dawn of history, the culture of the Seven Stars, has

Seven-story stone pagoda (Goryeo Dynasty, Unjusa Temple, Korea)

Seven-story stone pagoda (Goryeo Dynasty, Unjusa Temple, Korea)

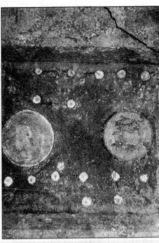

① A Painting of the Seven Gods of Longevity
(Joeseon Dynasty, National Folk Museum of Korea)

② Chilseong Yeorea: Seven Tathagatas of the Big Dipper
(Joseon Dynasty, Seonmun University Museum)

③ The Sun, the Moon, and the Seven Stars with the pole star.
(5 CE Goguryeo Dynasty, Jangcheon Tomb No.1)

①	②	③

The Seven Stars of the Northern Dipper on the Dolmen
in Korea

The Bottom Board of a Coffin with seven holes
representing the Seven Stars (14c. Joseon)

spread throughout the entire world. In Sumeria, the origin of Western civilization, they worshipped seven main Gods. This must have been connected to the Seven Stars at some point because the Sumerians are said to have come from across the Tianshan Mountains.

The present-day 7-day week calendar system also traces back to the Seven Stars culture of Hwanguk, humanity's first nation, 9,000 years ago.

The biggest way that we can see the pervasiveness of the culture of the Seven Stars, however, is by examining the pervasiveness of the topknot worn in the early cultures of the world.

The Topknot Revered the Seven Stars

Raising your hair into a topknot on your head was the very first hairstyle of humanity--not only in the East, but also all over the world. The kings of the East, West, and all civilizations wore topknots to revere the Seven Stars and receive energy from them. This is further evidence that the culture of the Seven Stars is the prototype culture from which all human ways of life originated.

The kings of the Sumerian civilization wore topknots. Shakyamuni of India (the founder of Buddhism) also raised his hair with a topknot. Sargon the Great, the King of Akaad, Kish and Sumer, is depicted with a topknot. Ancient Mayan figures are found with topknots. Native Americans wore the topknot. There is archaeological evidence that the people in Africa wore the topknot. When you visit the famous underground museum in Thailand, which exhibits cultural treasures of Ayutthaya kingdom, you'll find that all the buddha statues have a topknot.

Of course, even in Korea today the topknot is considered by many people to be a vestige of an outdated and uncivilized culture. The people of both the East and West have lost the connection with their primordial culture. But recently in Korea there has been a resurgence of this style among women making their hair into a topknot.

But rather than simply dismissing this as an uncivilized practice,

① Sargon, the Great of Akkad with a topknot (from 4,300 years ago)
② Sargon, the II of the Akkad Dynasty with a topknot.
③ A Statue of the Shakyamuni Buddha with a topknot (Government Museum, Mathura, India)
④ Buddhist statues wearing topknots (Ayuthaya Museum, Thailand)
⑤ A Blackfoot Indian's Topknot
⑥ A photograph of people in Africa wearing topknots (Museum of African Art, Korea)

we must ask ourselves, why did all the people of antiquity use topknots to raise their hair in this way, as if they had made an agreement or shared a unified culture? Given what we know about these early cultures it is clear that they did not simply make "fashion statements." They would only have adopted such a hairstyle if there were some purpose, some meaning.

The symbolic meaning of the topknot has been lost in many regions but we can learn about the meaning from the Korean word for topknot, which is *Sangtu*. *Sangtu* is an old word for the Seven Stars. People at that time understood that by tying their hair in this way they were connecting with the Seven Stars. To do this, the knot was made in a very specific way. They twisted their hair around seven times--four times to the front and three times backward--and then bound it together.

Raising one's hair into a *Sangtu* is a ritual that honors this fact that the Seven Stars are our original home and life source. It signifies a commitment to live in a sacred way, with one mind, uniting us with our ancestors and with God the Father. It symbolized the people's steadfast and awakened mind in connection with the seven stars, as if they were adjusting an antenna to tune into a radio frequency. It's a way of re-aligning ourselves with the direction of the north pole, the seven stars. It is the direction that the energy of enlightenment comes from. Just as when we are lost we can look at the Seven Stars and see where North is, so we can find who we are and return to our true self.

The idea that the Seven Stars confer power to humans may sound unscientific to modern readers, but recently there has been an amazing discovery related to this.

Science Validates the Power of the Seven Stars

Modern technology has produced an explanation for the secret of the Seven Stars in the northern sky, lending powerful support to the idea that Seven Stars is the source of human life and is the place that human beings return to when they die.

Since 2008, a collaboration of five countries, South Korea, the United States, Japan, Russia and Belgium, have overseen the largest observatory for ultra-high energy cosmic rays in the northern hemisphere, known as Telescope Array. Located in the desert of Utah, the project is equipped with three fluorescence telescopes and 507 scintillation surface detectors. The research team has been focused on detecting the ultra-high energy cosmic rays that are released in the universe.

Their astonishing discovery was that between May 11, 2008 and May 4, 2013 the astrophysicists detected 72 ultra-high energy cosmic rays and a full quarter of these rays came from a certain spot (right ascension 146.6 degrees and a declination 43.2 degrees) which makes up only about 6% of the sky. That is to say that these ultra-high energy cosmic rays were emitted from beneath the Big Dipper, the constellation Ursa Major. The research was accepted for publication by *Astrophysical Journal Letters*. Perhaps this added scientific research will open people's minds to the possibility that there is something true about this ancient understanding of the Seven Stars.

The Seven Star Mantra: Chil-seong-gyeong

The *Taeeulju* Mantra is the mantra that venerates *Taeeulchun Sangwongunnim* and is therefore the most important and powerful mantra. Taeeul means the the ultimate beginning, the ultimate origin, or the ultimate unity. However, there is another mantra, *Chil-seong-gyeong*, that conveys the meaning of Seven Stars. This mantra reveals the secret of the creation of human beings. This mantra sings of the original realization of the primordial culture, before the advent of Confucianism, Buddhism, Taoism and Christianity. The mantra entreats the Seven Stars to bestow upon the chanter the great *qi* of the universe and bless the practitioner with health and eternal life.

Here is the Seven Stars Mantra:

Chil-seong-yeo-rae Dae-je-gun Buk-du-gu-jin Jung-cheon-dae-sin Sang-jo-geum-gwol Ha-bu-gon-lyun Jo-ri-gang-gi Tong-je-geon-gon

Dae-goe-tam-rang Geo-mun-nok-jon Mun-gok-yeom-jeong Mugok-pa-gun

Go-sang-ok-hwang Ja-mi-je-gun Dae-ju-cheon-je Se-ip-mi-jin

Ha-jae-bul-myeol Ha-bok-bu-jin Won-hwang-jeong-gi Nae-hap-a-sin

Cheon-gang-so-ji Ju-ya-sang-ryun Sok-geo-so-in

(birth year) saeng (name) ho-do-gu-ryeong

Won-gyeon-jon-ui Yeong-bo-jang-saeng Sam-tae-heo-jeong Yuk-sun-gok-saeng

Saeng-a Yang-a Ho-a Hyeong-a Heo-sin-hyeong

Goe-Jak-Gwan-Haeng Hwa-Bo-Pyo Jon-Je-geup-geup Yeo-yul-ryeong

The mantra goes through the name of each star and the meaning of them. Each star has its own energy associated to it, and it gives its energy to our physical bodies. Within the mantra there is a section where you speak your name and your birth year and so you are placing yourself in the stars as well.

The Seven Star Mantra deals with nine stars as it includes the phrase Bukdu gujin, or the northern nine stars. As mentioned briefly before, the Big Dipper is actually consisted of nine stars, not seven stars. Apart from the northern nine stars, this mantra mentions Samtae-seong, literally meaning the three stars. To understand the complete teaching of the Chil-seong-gyeong mantra, it is important to know a bit about these as well. They are also known the Three

The Seven Stars and The Three Enclosures

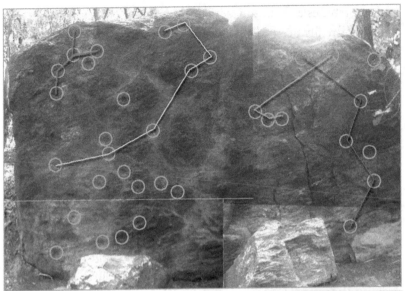

The Seven Stars and The Three Enclosures engraved on a Dolman in Korea.

A Painting of the sages of three enclosures. (Joseon Dynasty, Seonmun Univesrity Museum)

Stars, or the Three Enclosures. It is understood that the Seven Stars bestow the body to all human beings and the Three Stars give us our spirits. The Seven Stars and the *Samtaeseong* are a yin and yang pair.

In Korea, there is a very famous phrase that sums up the idea of these seven and three: *sam-hon-chil-baek.* That means, "The spirit works in three, and the soul works in seven." The idea is that inside us we all have three spirits and seven souls. Western cultures do not have a proper word to translate this particular spiritual terminology *hon, baek.* It has been translated sometimes as spirit and sometimes as soul, sometimes as heavenly soul and sometimes as earthly soul, but this is not really accurate. The problem is that the concept of *baek* doesn't exist in the West due to the prominent roles Heaven and God have played in shaping their worldview over thousands of years.

The essential point of the inclusion of the Three Enclosures, however, is that our bodies and souls are connected with heavenly stars. Heavenly soul and earthly soul are both important and part of the makeup of who we are. And they need to be in balance. The *Chil-seong-gyeong* mantra meditation is a process of clearing our three spirits and our seven souls. This corrects the imbalance and disharmony of the human body, mind, and spirit. It opens the doors of the mind to make health and longevity possible. All of the blessings and grace you have experienced throughout all of your life come from the Seven Stars. In essence the mantra therefore means, "I pray for the profound energy of heaven and earth to descend upon my body."

Within the mantra you also find eight syllables that are connected to the eightfold path. The basis of Buddhist meditation is the Eightfold Path which includes; right speech, right action, right livelihood, right effort, right mindfulness, right concentration, right view, and right resolve. What the Eightfold Path aims to achieve, can be achieved through chanting these 8 syllables: *Wun-Hwang-Jeong-Gi-Nae-Hap-Ah-Shin*. Let's chant it together; *Wun-Hwang-Jeong-Gi-Nae-Hap-Ah-Shin*.

元皇正氣 來合我身

Won-hwang-jeong-gi Nae-hap-a-sin

May the primordial and proper *qi* of heaven and earth come and unite with my body.

Chapter 3
The Second Gate to Enlightenment: The Culture of Tae-il, the Ultimate One

To pass through the second gate of enlightenment is to gain an understanding of the Ultimate One, known as *Tae-il* or the *Tae-il* human, which is the most sublime and divine being that makes the dream of Heaven and Earth come true.* At the core of the *Taeeulju* Mantra is the phrase *Tae-eul-cheon Sang-won-gun*. What this phrase is saying is that the central spirit of the *Taeeulju* Mantra is *Sang-won-gun*, he who resides in the *Tae-eul-cheon* heaven of the northern sky, which is the Star of *Tae-il*, known in the West as the Pole Star. The North Star is the central pivot point in the sky and the people of the three major countries of the Far East worshipped this star from long ago.

Tae-il means the highest king, the highest or heavenly king. In this very place resides the utmost, the highest being. Yes, in *Tae-il*, there is indeed the ultimate one who even the Lord *Sangjenim* of Seven Stars respects and prays to. There is a yin-yang relationship between the Northern Seven Stars and the Pole Star. The awakening of the Dao, or enlightenment, comes from both sides: The Seven Stars and the *Tae-eul-cheon* heaven. Before a person can

> * *Taeeul* and *Tae-il* means the same thing. They are interchangeable. *Taeeul* means the ultimate origin and *Tae-il* means the ultimate one. So the ultimate one is the ultimate origin.

become enlightened, both *Sangjenim* and *Sang-won-gun* must both affirm that the person is ready. When a seeker's dao and virtue reach full maturity, he or she will be summoned by the Holy Sovereign *Tae-eul* God.

The Message of All Enlightened Sages is Tae-il

Tae-il signifies the ultimate human being who has become one with the universal parents, Heaven and Earth. This refers to the highest level of awakening and enlightenment. It is the mind that has become one with the universe. Throughout all of history, there have been only a handful of awakened individuals who have come to know *Tae-il*. Those who achieve the purpose of Heaven and Earth, the ones who have achieved the great mind, who have been truly awakened, are referred to as *Tae-il*. They have attained a true ascension to humanity's majesty.

What is the ultimate path of enlightenment? The secret is in living our lives in union with the one mind of the fatherly Heaven and motherly Earth, the parents of all humanity and the wellspring of all of our lives. All people are born as children of Heaven and Earth.

We can find the concept of oneness in all the religions and sages of the East and West. In Confucianism it is said, "Focus with one mind

The Birth of the Taeeulju Mantra
- The Second Gate of Enlightenment:
The Culture of the Ultimate Great One

Taeilseong Star- Polaris

to maintain the middle path." In Buddhism they are taught to ask the question, "All dharmas return to one, but where does that one dharma return to?" In Taoism they believe that there is one ultimate energy of creation and transformation of the universe. In Christianity, Christ said, "I and the Father are one." In the Psalms of the Hebrew Bible (3:3) this realization is expressed in the statement, "But you, Lord, are a shield around me, my glory, the One who lifts my head high."

Today, the world has been torn apart by disorder, conflict, and division, but this can be turned around. Living in the Dao of *Tae-il* will open the gates of harmony, for this was the way life that was lived in humanity's first primordial culture. When people achieve the Dao of *Tae-il*, all of humanity will come together with one mind, as one human family. So today, we must drastically change our consciousness and our way of thinking to change the direction of human history. This calls for a culture of spirituality to begin.

The Tae-il Shrines in Korea, China, and Japan

The teaching of *Tae-il* goes back to the very beginning of the history of the East and you can find the remnants of this all throughout Korea, China, and Japan. In Japan, all shrines have their origin in the Seven Stars and the *Tae-il* star. There are four pillars

Taeilsa Temple Signboard (Nagano, Japan) which reads Temple of the Gods of the Northern Dipper

standing at the entrance to the Suwa Shinto temple, representing the first four of the Seven Northern Stars.

At the Suwa temple, every 7 years they conduct a Matsuri of erecting a pillar. All minds are spiritually raised through this ritual. They chant "Suwa!" Does it not sound like a Korean word "Sewa!" This sounds very much like the Korean word that means to make it proper or erect, or "set up." They are chanting, "Set up! Set up your mind! Set your mind upright!" They are erecting the mind to correct

Taeilsa Temple (Northern Dipper Shrine)

Sacred Pillars of the Main Shrine of Suwa Taisha

the mind. The mind has been faulted and they are straightening it out. "Straighten out your mind that has fallen wayside, erect your diseased mind, set up all the minds in the world!" Why would the Japanese be chanting a Korean word? Because the custom is part of their worship of Tae-il, which came from ancient Korea.

Near Suwa Temple upon a hill, there is a Tae-il Temple. Climbing a staircase, I found a stone monument that read, "Tae-il Temple." When I saw that, I knew that I had stumbled upon a hidden truth.

Taeil Matsuri (Isejingu Shrines)

Onbashira Festival, Suwa Taisha Matsuri

Taeil Matsuri (Isejingu Shrines)

The inspiration behind the Japanese Shinto temple was nothing less than *Tae-il*.

We can also see this archetypal culture in another historical site in Japan, the Ise Shrine. This is the headquarters of a hundred thousand Shinto shrines of Japan. The spirits of the Seven Stars are revered in the Outer Shrine of the temple and in the Inner Shrine they worship the spirit of *Tae-il*. They use the name *Tae-il Matsuri* and they conduct a massive ritual for Tae-il every year. They disassemble and rebuild the temple and when they do, they cut off the main pillar and and this main pillar symbolizes Tae-il. In this way, they erect *Tae-il* every twenty years when they rebuild the temple. The ceremony symbolizes the mind of the Father in the Northern sky, the one mind of *Tae-eul-cheon Sang-won-gun*, who resides in the *Tae-il* Heavenly Palace. All minds are spiritually raised through this ritual.

Emperor Wu of Han (156 BCE -87 BCE), The 7th Emperor of the Han Dynasty of China

Emperor Wu of Han dynasty built the Taeil Altar and offered Heavenly Rites to the Taeil Spirit.

You can also find the prevalence of the culture of *Tae-Il* in ancient China. According to the most famous historian of China, Sima Qian, in *The Record of the Grand Historian*, "Heavenly one, Earthly one, Supreme one." What could be meant by this cryptic phrase? This is speaking of the original form of the culture of *Tae-Il*. A human being is the one that fulfills and accomplishes the will of heaven and earth. Those humans who accomplish this are, therefore, called the ultimate one, the *Tae-il*. We will return to this idea in a moment when we explore the ancient scripture that Sima Qian must have gained this insight through.

Qu Yuan (340BCE -278 BCE), a Poet from the State of Chu

In Northern China, 2,200 years before Sima Qian wrote his profound statement, the emperor Wu of Han defeated the Xiongnu of Northern China. He then built an altar in the Southeastern section of the palace where he offered rituals to the spirit of *Tae-Il*.

Koreans have preserved this teaching for the past ten thousand years in many ways since Korea is the origin of the culture of *Tae-il*. A marvelous quote revealing the foundation of Eastern culture is from

東皇太一

Donghwang-Taeil

"The Emperor of the East is Tae-il."
Qu Yuan is saying that the Emperor of the East
was the Ultimate One, known as Tae-il.

the poet Qu Yuan (340-278 BCE) of the Chu dynasty of China. The quote is actually the title of his first poem, "The Emperor of the East is *Tae-il*." He is saying that the Emperor of the East was the Ultimate One, known as *Tae-il*. You know the origin of Eastern cultures if you understand what this means. Qu Yuan says that the original source of Eastern Culture is neither China nor India, but the land to their East, which was ancient Korea.

Nammyung JoShik (1501-1572) was a Confucian scholar during the Joseon Dynasty. In his work, *Shin-myung-ah-myung*, he referred to the body as a country where the mind resides and the mind is the capital of that country. He revealed that our mind is the lord and sovereign of *Tae-il*.

We can actually meet *Tae-il* in the United States, in the Boston Museum of Fine Arts. He is called the Buddha of Blazing Lights (*Chi-sung-gwang-yeo-rae*) in Buddhism. In Daoism, he has been called the *Taeeul* spirit, *Taeeul-Gugo- Cheonjon*. The Buddha of Blazing Lights is the Buddha burning in the light and flame of the holy spirit of the

The Sovereign of Taeil

Nammyeong Josik revealed
that our mind is the lord and
sovereign of Tae-il.

Nammyeong Josik (1501-1572,
A Confucian Scholar of Joseon
Dyansty)

grand universe. When we look at this painting, which is originally from Korea(Goryeo Dynasty, late 14th century), we see the sitting Buddha, who is known in Sanskrit as *Tejaprabha*. The North Pole is his chariot. In the picture, there are sixteen bodies of bodhisattvas in front of him. Who are these sixteen Buddhas? They are eight yins and eight yang. The idea is that all the energy of enlightenment is coming from this Polaris, from *Taeeulcheon Sangwongun*, the *Tae-il*, the *Taeeul* spirit. When you chant the mantra of *Taeeulcheon Sangwongun* for some time and receive higher levels of teachings, your realization deepens, and you will see that the secret truth of the universe is contained within this picture.

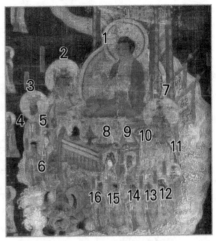

The Descent of Tejaparbha Buddha, the Lord Taeeul of the pole star (14c. Goryeo Dynasty, Museum of Fine Arts Boston)

Yeongyeongdang Hall of Changdeokgung Palace (The gate of taeil))

In the Yeongkyeong Court, inside the Changdeok Palace built during the Joseon Dynasty of Korea, the Tae-il gate still stands today.

When you visit the Tae-eul Rock in Tae Ahn County, on the west coast of Korea, you will find the words, Tae-Eul-Dong-Cheon, inscribed on it.

The Heavenly Code

The understanding of *Tae-il* first surfaces in the original scripture of the East, the *Cheonbugyeong*, which means The Heavenly Code Scripture. This scripture has never been properly introduced to the world, but there are at least one hundred papers and books written about this text in Korea. The *Cheonbugyeong* is a short scripture of only 81 characters. It has been recited like a mantra for thousands of years. It is a very short scripture, but it contains the principles of the universe and the meaning of human life through a teaching of sacred numerology.

According to records, the *Cheonbugyeong* was originally passed down orally in the Eastern nation of Hwanguk, the first nation ever established by humanity in the Tianshan Mountains in Central Asia, 9,000 years ago. Some people argue whether it has existed from the

Taeeuldongcheon (Taeeulam Hermitage, Taean County)

very beginning of time. It was recorded by Shinji Hyeokdeok of the Baedal dynasty (3897-2333 BCE) using Nokdomun, the ancient hieroglyphic characters. Around 4,000 years ago, it was inscribed on a boulder and erected on Taebaksan mountain, by the Shinji of Dangun Joseon. The Dangun Joseon dynasty was from 2333-239 BCE. Around 1,000 years ago, the great scholar of the Unified Silla Dynasty, Choe Chi-won (857-908 CE), discovered a stone monument, that had the *Cheonbugyeong* engraved on it. He translated it using the hanja characters that we use today and revealed it to the world. He also engraved the *Cheonbugyeong* scripture on a stone in Myohyangsan mountain in its honor and set up a monument.

The word *Cheonbu* means that it is the law of the heavens, or

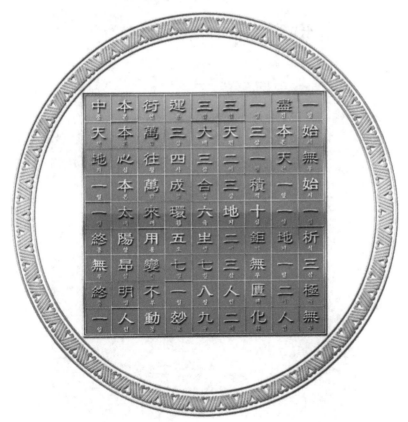

Cheonbugyeong, The Scripture of Heavenly Code

God's mandate. There are some Chinese scholars who have grasped the significance of this text. A scholar by the name of Zhu Wie Li stated that there are at least 10 separate and distinct renderings for the term 'heavenly code.' Among others, he has defined them as heavenly law, heavenly principle, and heavenly mandate.

All the teachings about human beings in Eastern culture have their roots in the teachings of the *Cheonbugyeong*. It is the original teaching of the numerology of cosmic creation that *Sangjenim* bestowed unto humanity. In the process of examining these sacred teachings, sages and wise men of the East and West came to realize many cosmic principles. The realization and systematizing of the

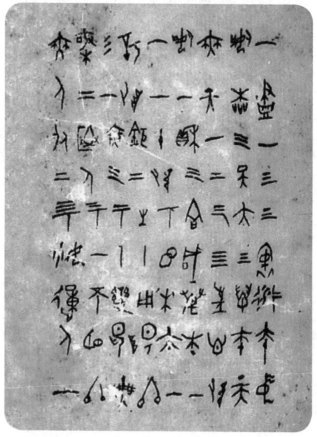

Cheonbugyeong

cosmic principle using basic numbers led to the blossoming of the *I Ching* (with 64 hexagrams), the *Ho Tu* (Hado, known as the diagram of mutual life-bettering and life-saving), *Lo Shu* (Nakseo, known as the magic square), and Right Change (Jeong Yuk). It is the codification of yin and yang, the 12 animals that are in the Zodiac, the 12-month cycle, and the 60 years cycle. It is the codification of herbal medicine. It is also the foundation of what we would

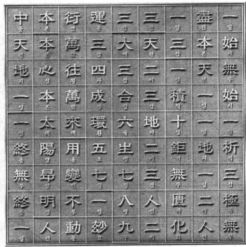

The Cheonbugyeong develope into the Cosmic 1 year.

Cheonbugyeong

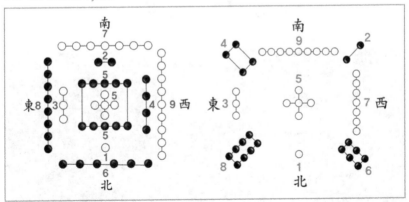

Hado and Nakseo; Ho Tu (Hado, known as the diagram of mutual life-bettering and life-saving), Lo Shu (Nakseo, known as the magic square of mutual conflict and domination).

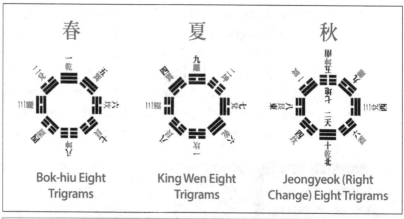

春	夏	秋

Bok-hiu Eight Trigrams

King Wen Eight Trigrams

Jeongyeok (Right Change) Eight Trigrams

The Cosmic Year
우주 1년

50,000 years Later Heaven

Winter

Early Heaven Gaebyeok

Rest 藏

Harvest 斂

Autumn

Birth 生

Spring

Growth 長

Later Heaven Gaebyeok

Summer

Early Heaven 50,000 years

the Early Heaven and Later Heaven

call oriental philosophy. The teachings of Taoism by Lao Tzu are probably the closest thing known in the West to the teaching of the *Cheonbugyeong*. Out of this also came the five elements of Confucism, the chakras of the body, and the acupuncture points.

The *Cheonbugyeong* was first revealed in the United States by Dr. Hongbeom Rhee. He calls the *Cheonbugyeong* the "Heaven Given Bible" and says that all spiritual thoughts and ideas of the East and the West came from the *Cheonbugyeong*. He confirms that the people of ancient Korea compiled the *Cheonbugyeong* and that its teachings were then transmitted to China, Japan, and even Europe. In his book, *Asian Millenarianism*, Dr. Rhee summarized his research findings. It is said that President Obama read this book and it played a part in altering his views on China.

Before we examine this ancient text in more detail, let me give you the full translation so that you can experience it yourself. Remember that only when we meditate on the *Cheonbugyeong* very sincerely for our whole life can we truly translate this mysterious code.

One cosmic year is 129,600 years on Earth.

- The principle of mutual conflict and domination is the source of all bitterness and grief.
- It is the source of the origin of sin.

Where does humanity currently stand?

- The transition period between the cosmic summer and cosmic autumn.
- The fundamental order of autumn: Now is the time to return the origin and one's own root (ancestors)

The Cheonbugyeong
Translation by the Jeung San Do Research Institute

One is the beginning; from Nothingness begins One.
One divides into the Three Ultimates, yet remains an
inexhaustible source.
Arising from One, Heaven is One.
Arising from One, Earth is Two.
Arising from One, Humanity is Three.
One accumulates and climaxes at Ten, as Three governs the
change of all things.
Based on Two, Heaven changes under Three.
Based on Two, Earth changes under Three.
Based on Two, Humanity lives under Three.
The Great Three unite into Six, which then gives rise to Seven,
Eight, and Nine.
Everything moves in accordance with Three and Four; everything
circulates under Five and Seven.
One proliferates in mysterious ways, evolving in perpetual cycles,
and these functions ultimately transform into immutable
substance.
The basis of the universe is the mind, which shines radiantly like
the sun.
Humanity, united with Heaven and Earth, attains the Ultimate
Oneness.
One is the end; in Nothingness ends One.

The Numerology of Heaven, the Earth and Humanity

There are 81 characters in the *Cheonbugyeong* and 70% of them
are numbers. It is the original scripture of sacred numerology, of
cosmic mathematics. It explains the secrets of the universe and
humanity using the numbers one through ten. The most important
numbers are one, three, and six. The number one appears eleven

times in the text, the number three appears eight times, and the number six appears in the exact center of the text.

The *Cheonbugyeong* is a way of expressing the cycle of life, and thus the cycle of the universe. It is a way of speaking about how the human body is made, how we grow up, how we mature, and the meaning of life. In the beginning, there was one but it is a beginningless one. One symbolizes the ultimate existence, the origin of the universe, and the foundation of all living things. The number one also represents Dao, God, or the Creator. The number one indicates that all things in the universe come from the same source. All things come from one, but this one comes from nothingness. This oneness is also *Tae-il*, the ultimate oneness or *Taeeul*, the ultimate origin of nothingness.

We can think of two as in units, or we can think of two as the second, or we can think of it as dividing into two. We can think of it as the step of growth that leads to life. Three represents life. If there are two, then they can give birth to a third, so three is birth and beginning.

The number three relates directly to the lesson of *Tae-il*. The number one self-manifests to the three ultimate beings, or the three ultimates of heaven, earth, and humanity. All three of them contain equal divinity as the Creator. They are known as the heavenly one, the earthly one, and the humanly one, or the ultimate one. These three, Heaven, Earth, and humanity, contain the ultimate divinity of the universe, but the humans are the hands of the creation-transformation power of the creator. Human beings are not just creatures of creation. We are active in the creation and un-creation of the cosmos. Human beings are the ones who achieve the dream and thoughts of their ultimate parents, Heaven and Earth. Because of this, people are even nobler than Heaven and Earth. They are the living God in the phenomenal realm. It is we who attain the fulfillment of the designs of Heaven and Earth.

This profound teaching comes from the ideology of the three ultimates. Heaven and Earth are in place of God and they take on the roles of the father and mother of humanity. Humanity came into being through the power of the creation-transformation of heaven and earth. Humans are the most dignified form of being and achieve the will and the ideology of God. Human beings are not just a mere creation. Human beings can use the hand of God in the realm of God and bring harmony to Heaven, Earth and humanity, thereby achieving the ultimate purpose of the will of God and the principle of the universe. The process for achieving that is meditation practiced with faith and devotion.

When a life is born and grows up, it comes into who it is, becomes aware of the meaning of the self and that is maturation, or number four, coming to fruition. Four is the number for autumn, the harvest time in the process of birth, growth, harvest, and rest. In this cycle in nature, the seasons come whether we want them to or not. But the point is that we begin to ask what is the meaning of our lives? We want to harvest our lives. We want to find meaning in our lives. It can be compared to that of a farmer. When autumn comes, the farmer harvests, and things come into fruition.

That is the cycle of 1,2,3,4. These numbers also refer to many other things. One is the direction of north and the color is black. Two is the direction of South and the color is red. Three is the direction East and the color blue. Four is the direction West and the color white. One is represented by the turtle, two by the phoenix, three by the dragon, and four by the tiger. One represents winter, two represents summer, three represents spring, and four represents autumn. One is the energy of water, two is the energy of fire, three is the energy of tree or life, four is the energy of metal.

Now, when I harvest my life, then I am again involved. That I am the number five. I am the one who is harvesting my life. The process of arriving at that is what meditation is. Through meditation we reverse the energy and return to the source. In that contracting process, I am the one who is returning home, to my roots, harvesting spring and summer, and understanding the meaning of my life. I do this in meditation.

The way water flows in trees in the different seasons is a helpful analogy. In the winter, the water in the trees returns to the ground, to the roots. In springtime, it goes through the tree and makes leaves. In summer, the water goes out to the leaves, and the leaves multiply and the trees grow. When autumn comes, the leaves dry and the nutrients go to the fruit and the trees bear fruits. Then the water goes back into the ground. The water needs to go back to the roots when winter comes. Otherwise the trees freeze and die. Because the water returns to the roots the trees live. The point of human life is that we are born and we grow up, but we have this feeling of emptiness or this sense that we must see who we are. We have this need to understand the meaning of life. That is the autumn of humanity and of life, the time of maturity, and the time of returning to our roots.

Now we arrive at the number six, which may be the most important number for our time. This has to do with a verse in the *Cheonbugyeong* that clearly shows us why the *Taeeulju* Mantra is the most important and the holiest mantra. This verse also illustrates why its healing life energy is the most powerful energy that has been revealed in the last 10,000 years of the history of the evolution of human civilization. The verse says, *Dae-sam-ham-yuk*. This means that when humanity becomes one mind and one body with Heaven and Earth, the cosmic parents, the water of eternal life comes down to us. This is represented by the number six.

The number six occurs when the number five connects with the number one, when the enlightened self comes in touch with the energy of water. This is why the number six is in the center of the *Cheonbugyeong*. The *Taeeulju* Mantra gives us the eternal water energy that is represented by the number six so that we may become the beings of *Tae-il*. The blessing of enlightenment that is attained through meditation is that humanity becomes reawakened. This is the will of the universe and the purpose of human life. The water of life is also referred to in Christianity. "How can a man be born when he is old? Verily, verily, I say unto thee, except a man be born of water and of the Spirit, he cannot enter into the kingdom of God." (Book of John 3:4-5)

When Heaven, Earth, and their children, humanity, unite to become one mind and one embodiment, the sum is six. The number six is also formed from the union of one, two, and three. So six symbolizes all of the meaning of one, two, and three. Heaven's one is one, Earth's one is two, humanity's one is three. So it represents Heaven, Earth, and humanity all coming together. It represents the achievement of the purpose of human life. But it is only humanity that does this, who is able to accomplish this. This is the ultimate lesson of *Tae-il* and the purpose of the the *Taeeulju* Mantra. But to really embrace this gift, you must understand why it is so urgent that we as a people develop this practice now, at this moment in time.

Chapter 4

The Third Gate of Enlightenment:

The Rise of the Eastern Learning Movement and the Coming of the Cosmic Autumn

The third and final gate of enlightenment brings us into the hidden history of modern-day Korea. So far, we have discussed the hidden ancient history of Northeast Asia, but there is also much in the modern history that has been neglected and distorted. This is the story of the Eastern Learning Movement, which is a missing link in our modern history. The ancient teachings declared that the Heavenly Father Himself would come down to the land of Korea, and this occurred at the end of the 19th century.

The Eastern Learning Movement started in preparation for the coming of the Heavenly Father Sangjenim to this earth, and the later movement begun by Sangjenim Himself had a tremendous impact on Korean society. For reasons that will soon be clear, they have not been studied well by historians and sociologists. The teachings of Sangjenim are the culmination of 9,000 years of Korean culture, but these teachings are important for the entire world because the predictions of the Eastern Learning Movement are becoming more and more relevant each day. The world must take note of this message so that it can be prepared for the Cosmic Autumn that is upon us.

Preparation for the Incarnation of Sangjenim

The story of the incarnation of Sangjenim in Korea actually begins with a Jesuit priest named Matteo Ricci (1552-1610) who came to China to spread Christianity. He learned Chinese and became so well versed in the language that wealthy Chinese people sent their sons to be tutored by him. Ricci discovered that all the leading Chinese scholars were Confucian, so he studied and translated the teachings of Confucianism. In fact, some people claim his translations became the birth of the age of Enlightenment because of their focus on logic and reasoning. It was one of the stepping stones that enabled Europe to come out of the dark ages. In particular, it inspired Leibnitz, one of the earliest Enlightenment thinkers, with a binary system.

When Ricci translated the teachings of Christianity into Chinese, he translated the word God as Sangjenim. To introduce the Chinese people to Christianity he wrote a book called *The True Meaning of the Heavenly Lord.* In that book, he shows that originally Confucianism was focused on the worship of Sangjenim. They understood Him to be the ruling governor of the universe, from Whom came the

(Left) The portrait of the venerable Mateo Ricci(1552-1610). He has bestowed the greatest virtue to humanity. (Right) His tombstone in Beijing

principle of the Universe, and they believed that He governed by becoming one with the principle of the Universe. Ricci shows how Confucianism later went away from Sangjenim and focused instead on the principles of the universe. Ricci argued that now the important thing was to again combine the principles of the Universe with God through Christianity. Through Ricci's book, Christianity gained some initial followers in China. Later, however, the Pope made it unacceptable to call God by the name Sangjenim.

Ricci's book, *The True Meaning of the Heavenly Lord*, was released in Korea and became a bestseller. Although it was not at all Ricci's intent, the book became the basis of Neo-Confucianism in Korea, which sought to re-establish the worship of Sangjenim. This movement in Korea laid the groundwork for the growth of the Eastern Learning Movement.

The True Meaning of the Heavenly Lord authored by Matteo Ricci

The Enlightenment of Choe Su-un

In the late 19th century, the tempest of Western Imperialism stormed throughout the world. European nations colonized Africa, the Americas, and South Asia and then turned to the last unconquered territory, Northeast Asia. Korea, known as Joseon at the time, stood on the brink of chaos. At that time, a seeker named Choe Su-un (1824-1864) prayed to Sangjenim to find the true dharma that would save the world

The Venerable Su-un, Choe Je-u (1824-1864)

from such madness. But his efforts initially bore no fruit. Then, on the 5th day of the lunar April, in 1860, a miraculous event happened. Su-un received the heavenly mandate in *Gyeongju*, the city that was once the capital of Silla, the thousand-years kingdom.

Sangjenim said, "Do not fear. Do not be alarmed. I am the one who people call Sangjenim. Do you not know Sangjenim? I am giving you the eternal and boundless dao. Meditate with it, write about

The Yongdamjeong Temple. The venerable Choe Su-un heard Sangjenim's voice on lunar April 5th, 1860 after 49 days of meditation in this location. The Yongdamjeong Temple is located at the Gumisan Mountain, Gyeongju City.

it, and then teach others. If you establish the path to this truth and spread virtue, you will live long and your name will shine brightly throughout the world." (Jeung San Do Dojeon 1:7)

Su-un then heard Sangjenim say, "Receive this mantra." This is the mantra that Su-un shared with his followers in anticipation of the coming of Sangjenim:

Shee-chun-ju Jo-hwa-jung Yung-seh-bool-mahng Mahn-sa-jee

"Serve the Lord of Heaven, who comes to the world in person and decides creative change. Never forget the infinite grace that grants enlightenment about all matters."

Jee-ghee -geum-jee-wun-wee-dae-gahng

"Pray that the ultimate qi, the ripening qi of autumn, abundantly descends from above."

--Jeung San Do Dojeon 1:7

Shee-chun-ju mantra

Shee-chun-ju Jo-hwa-jung Yung-seh-bool-mahng Mahn-sa-jee

Jee-ghee -geum-jee-wun-wee-dae-gahng

At that time, Sangjenim gave Su-un enlightenment and the truth of Singyo, or the spiritual teaching. He received the heavenly mandate directly from the Father Sangjenim, who resides in the Northern Seven Stars, and founded Donghak, the Eastern Learning. This was a defining moment of a new culture of spirituality, a new beginning in the history of human civilization. This was the beginning of the modern history of humanity in the Korean Peninsula.

For five years Su-un announced to the world that Sangjenim Himself would soon come to Korea to usher in a new world of harmony. He was very popular with the people but, sadly, the Korean government was afraid of Su-un. Finally, they arrested and executed him. According to the official document, when he was being executed they were not able to kill him at first. The blade of the sword would not go through his neck. The executioner pleaded with Su-un to help him, and Su-un said that he was sorry but that he had a heavenly mandate. He told the executioner, that the only way it would be possible to kill him was if he offered a bowl of fresh water to Sangjenim and prayed to him; afterwards, he told his executioner, "Do not fear and cut my head off," only then the executioner was able to cut Su-un's head off.

They may have been able to kill Su-un, but they could not stop the movement that Su-un began. Donghak, or Eastern Learning, grew to more than three million followers. But they lived in a time of tyranny and corruption. In the year 1894, the cries of the people turned into a wide-scale revolution that spread like wildfire, with the goal of completely changing the history of Joseon forever.

The followers of Donghak chanted the mantra Su-un taught them and fought for equality, representation, and human rights against the corrupt government. It is estimated that a total of 600 thousand Koreans were involved with the Donghak revolution. They were claiming the coming of heaven, the later heaven. They didn't have proper weapons, but they were able to take over the state

수운이 상제님께 청수를 올린 후 형리에게 '안심하고 베라'고 하자 목이 베어졌다. 오지영 「동학사」 참조

Su-un offered a bowl of fresh water to Sangjenim and prayed to him; afterwards, he told his executioner, 'Do not fear and cut my head off,' only then the executioner was able to cut Su-un's head off.

government. When they advanced near the capital, Seoul, the Korean government was afraid and asked the Japanese to help.

The Japanese Imperial Army came into Korea and decimated the peasant army. This became the basis of the Japanese colonizing Korea. They killed the Eastern Learning revolutionaries mercilessly. The people were completely butchered, turing the Geumgang River red for six months. Still, the Eastern Learning Revolution was a cry of freedom under the name of Serving the Lord of Heaven and Earth. It was a movement that opened up a new paradigm in Korea. The revolution may have failed, but they could not suppress the teachings of Eastern Learning and the advent of Sangjenim.

The statue of the Maitreya Buddha (Middle)

The Incarnation of Sangjenim

Before he died, the final words the Sacred Venerable Choe Su-un said were, "It is late, it is late by eight years." Then, eight years after his death, in 1871, Sangjenim was incarnated as a human being to open the way of The Supreme Dao. Sangjenim Himself came to Korea from the Seven Stars of the Big Dipper, as predicted in the ancient teachings. He is understood to be the Heavenly Lord, the Father who is the same as the Maitreya Buddha, the Buddha of Hope, the Future Buddha.

Sangjenim declared, "The whole world is suffering from a monstrous disease. I am using My authority over the three realms and the power of creative change to open a new heaven and a new earth." (Jeung San Do Dojeon 2:12) And so he descended to earth, and Jeung San Do (the True Eastern Learning Movement) was born. At the time of the revolution, Sangjenim was still in his youth and did not take part. In fact during revolution, Sangjenim told his followers not to take up weapons. He started a spiritual undertaking, not a political revolution.

As a God himself with the coming of Cosmic Autumn harvest of humanity, he came to Earth as a human being to conduct the work

Taemo Go-subunim. (left) Seongdo-ri town. It is the birth place of Taemonim who received the dao lineage from Jeung San Sangjenim and and spread the first seeds of the dao affairs.

of harvesting humanity. All good deeds will bear fruits and all bad deeds must answer to bitter grief that it has caused. Thus, as a human being, he conducted the work of resolution of bitter grief upon human history. He provided an opportunity for humanity to resolve their bitter grief and harvest history so individual enlightenment might occur.

Part of Sangjenim's concern was over the deep grief women experience in this world. He saw that the world suffers from an imbalanced yin and yang. He said that as a result of this imbalance, "The natural course of heaven and earth is being blocked as they are filled with the bitterness and grief of women. From this, a disaster threatens to burst forth with the power to destroy the human world." (Jeung San Do Dojeon 2:33) He made it possible for there to be a coming age of equality, "when entrusting people with any work, there will be no discrimination between men and women." (Jeung San Do Dojeon 2:33)

Sangjenim didn't have a large religious movement. During his time he had only about 100 disciples or so, though he was

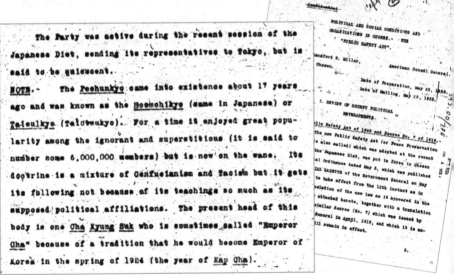

A CIA report stating that members of Bocheongyo was around 6 million people.

famous. It was only after he passed away that his wife created a movement and more people began to follow his teachings. Before he passed away, he passed down his enlightenment to his wife, Taemonim, because it is the age of Yin. Of course she also meditated in earnest to receive such enlightenment. It was under her leadership that the movement grew. Even though the actual movement was spearheaded by her cousin, it spread throughout Korea until as many as two-thirds of the Korean population were chanting the Taeeulju Mantra and following the teachings of Sangjenim. Unfortunately, the movement grew too much. According to Miller Report complied for USA defense department, up to 6 mllion people were adherents of the teaching. Although they were not planning a revolution, the Japanese government was afraid of the movement, so they persecuted and killed so many of the followers that the movement diminished again for some time.

The teaching survived, however, and has been reborn as Jeung San Do. With the liberation of Korea from Japanese rule, the Jeung San Do movement blossomed again and gained a large following. However, with the Korean war, the movement again went into hiding. The present day movement of Jeung San Do started to spread in Korea during the tumultuous 1980s when a number of my books

The book; *Gaebyeok; The Real Situation*

gained popularity. This was during a time in Korea's history when the foundation of Korean democracy and Korean economic development was taking shape. Because the teachings of the Jeung San Do emphasize the ideals of equality, democracy, and mutual life-bettering and life-saving, many people see my books as having laid the foundation for such a development. Jeung San Do completes the dream and realizes the ideals of the first Eastern Learning movement. The people of Joseon have awakened to the messages of Eastern

Learning and have gathered once again.

This is the historical background of Eastern Learning and Jeung San Do that continues to pave the way for the culture of the Taeeulju Mantra and the culture of Tae-il, the Ultimate One. To understand why this was inevitable and why it is so urgent that the world take note of this message, we turn once more to the *Cheonbugyeong* and examine the concept of the cosmic year.

The Cosmic Year

Knowledge about the Cosmic Year represents the final culmination of the 9,000 year lineage of enlightenment to the Cosmic principle. It originates from the *Cheonbugyeong*, which, as we have already seen, is the original form of the numerology and teachings of the cosmic creation that Sangjenim bestowed unto humanity.

In the latter half of the 19th century, after the proclamation of the arrival of the new cosmic history by Eastern Learning, the sacred, venerable Gim Il-bu completed *Jeongyeok* (Right Change, or Enlightenment Change) through lifelong devotion to self-cultivation. At that time, he revealed a diagram that completed the history of the cosmology of the East and the West. The cosmic year diagram contains the key to understanding the principle of heaven and earth to overcome the impending revolutionary changes of

The portrait of Kim Il-bu, The founder of the Jeong-yeok and his shrine, located in Southern Chuncheong Province.

春

Bok-hiu Eight Trigrams

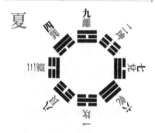

夏

King Wen Eight Trigrams

秋

Jeongyeok (Right Change)
Eight Trigrams

The venerable Kim Il-bu received a message
from the Heave and Earth after devoting his
entire life to the philosophy of Change. And
then, he draw the Eight Trigrams of Jeongyeok
(Right Change), thereby completing the I-Ching.

50,000 years
Later Heaven

Winter

Early Heaven
Gaebyeok

Rest
藏

ic Year

한수 1년

Harvest
斂

Birth
生

Autumn

Spring

Growth
長

Later Heaven
Gaebyeok

Early Heaven
50,000 years

Summer

gaebyeok, and to open the gates to the new history to come. And embracing the principle of *Jeongyeok,* Ahn Unsan, His Holiness the Taesang Jongdosanim of Jeung San Do, declared the great order of the creation-transformation of heaven and earth, and engraved the actual 129,600-year diagram of the cosmic year. It is known as the cosmic year diagram. The cosmic year diagram clearly and simply illuminates the principle of the creation-transformation of Heaven and Earth. It explains the birth of human civilization, the development of our societies, the state of the global society today, and the future of the world.

Just as there is one year on earth, there is a larger and grander scale of the cosmic year in the cosmos. The cosmic year is 129,600 earthly years long. We have a clear understanding now that in the

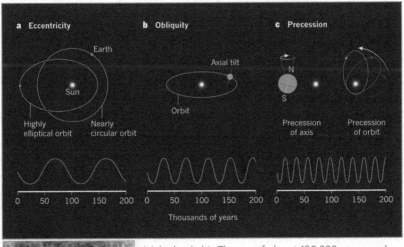

Mylankovitch's Theory of about 130,000 years cycle of one Cosmic Year.

The Portrait of Mylankovitch

past 10 million years or so we had great ice ages that came in cycles of about every 130,000 years. These ages became the major driving force behind the evolution of animals and humans. This is called the Mylankovitch cycle. It is named after the man who calculated that the Earth's orbit around the Sun changes from circular to elliptical in the cycle of about 100,000 years. Along with the orbital cycle, there is a shift in the tilt of the Earth's axis, which is about 40,000 years. And then there is the wobble of the axis in the cycle of about 20,000 years. In combinations of them, Mylankovitch calculated that it is the combined cycle of axis rotation of orbit, tilt and wobble that brings about the great ice age cycle of about 130,000 years.

Whether it's a cosmic year or an earthly year, the basic principle is the same: there are seasons of birth, growth, harvest and rest. These are the fundamental principles of the universe. Humanity was born fifty thousand years ago in this cosmic year. This marked the end of the last great ice age and the beginning of current humanity: the rise of Homo Sapiens and the demise of Neanderthals.

What is important to understand about this cosmic year is that we happen to be living at the extreme, at the edge of the cosmic summer and we are about to enter the cosmic autumn. These ideas were developed long ago, long before the understanding emerged about global warming, but they explain what is happening from a spiritual perspective. The debate over whether or not climate change is man-made misses the truth that humanity is also part of the natural cycle. Yes, we are causing global warming, but we are also part of nature and this is the result of human conflict during the time of growth in the cosmic summer.

Still, we need to recognize that we are about to enter into a new era. This is the time when the universe closes down and exits the season of the cosmic spring and summer and enters into the season of cosmic autumn. In the past, no saints, philosophers, religious leaders, or futurists could accurately understand the order of the cosmic cycle. This is the missing link to a proper understanding of who we are, where we are, and when we are existing.

The Coming of the Later Heaven and Mutual Life-Bettering and Life-Saving

The shift in cosmic seasons is brought about by a shift in the heavens. There exist two quite different heavens that raise human civilizations with different principles. There are the Early Heaven and the Later Heaven. The period from Cosmic Spring to Summer is called the Early Heaven 선천. The period from Cosmic Autumn to Winter is called the Later Heaven 후천.

The basic principle of Early Heaven is *Sanggeuk. Sanggeuk* means mutual restraint or mutual conflict. Since the purpose of the Early Heaven is to produce and grow humans and nature, the principle of competition and struggle is inevitable in the Early Heaven. As a result of the principle of mutual conflict and domination, all things on earth in the time of cosmic spring and summer develop in an imbalanced way. That's why even our pole is shifted in one direction. During the Early Heaven, the axis of the earth is tilted. Due to this tilt, we have extreme cold and extreme hot.

It is owed to the principle of mutual conflict and domination that we have conflicts and competition, which result in imbalance and disparity. This disparity and imbalance in economics is the cause of wars and various kinds of suffering in human societies, including fierce competition, regional conflicts, natural disasters, and endless wars. These are all derived from the *Sanggeuk* nature of Early Heaven. Because nature itself operates within such a Cosmic Principle of conflict, humanity lives under the environment of disparity and imbalance.

The important thing we must grasp is how to evolve beyond this age of conflict. The Later Heaven is dominated by the principle of *Sangsaeng*, mutual life-bettering and life-saving. This is a period that matures and unifies human civilization and nature. Therefore, eternal peace and harmony is accomplished in the Later Heaven. Until we understand this, we cannot go beyond the framework of the past thinking.

When we have advanced from the time of Cosmic Summer to the

Cosmic Autumn, all natural disasters and wars of the Early Heaven will end. We will enter a period of harmony and balance between nature and humanity. This new order of the Universe is *Sangsaeng*. What does *Sangsaeng* mean? *Sang* means mutual or each other. *Saeng* means to save or to benefit. Thus *Sang-Saeng* means to save each other and to benefit each other.

In the coming age, extreme cool and warm weather disappears from earth. Yin and yang energy comes into balance in nature and in civilization. Complete balance and harmony comes about and the order of oppressed yin and revered yang change to the order of equal yin and yang energy. Thus discrimination of women in the work force, unequal rights for women, the income gap between men and women—all these issues will be resolved and all natural disasters will end.

Sangjenim introduced a secret method called *uitong* to help us usher in this new era. Uitong means to unite humanity by healing. Humanity cannot become one unless and until the wrongs of the past that are paining humanity are healed. We cannot simply say, "Let's get together and hold hands." We have to rectify the wrongs of the past and heal the psychological wounds of the pains of the past as well. Otherwise they will generate physical illnesses in the people and societies that carry those pains.

To rectify the wrong means to correct the history. Holocaust museums are a good example of this. So is the apology by Japan to Korea's "comfort women" who were kept as sexual slaves by the Japanese. These are good starts, but afterward we need to heal the psychological wounds through meditation for the world to become truly one. For this we need the Taeeulju Mantra.

The main message of Eastern Learning is that the age of the heavenly Father is opening as the absolute infinite, the *Mu-geuk-dae-do*. As it is stated in the *Korean Dojeon*, "Now is the age of heaven and earth's achievement of their purpose." (Korean Dojeon 2:43) Now is the time of Cosmic Autumn, "The autumn destiny of all the world has now dawned" (Korean Dojeon 2:43) This is the most important message that Jeung San Do, has been conveying. The time of healing, the Cosmic Autumn, is coming. Nevertheless, we must also be aware that to change this world from the principle of mutual conflict and domination to the principle of mutual life-bettering and life-saving will not be easy. This point of great change is expressed in Korean as *Gaebyeok*.

The Great Change of Gaebyeok

The approaching time of *Gaebyeok* is when the universe and humanity will be reborn. *Gaebyeok* is the message of hope that humanity will encounter a new world. *Gaebyeok* is not the end, it is merely a message of hopeful new beginnings. However, this period of rebirth will also be a period of great upheaval. Although *Gaebyeok* is not the end, the transition to the time of Autumn is a period of great disaster and disease. The future does not come about through the advancement of new technology alone. All futurists claim the same thing. The disruption of modern civilization awaits us. "We are facing the end time. We cannot avoid *Gaebyeok*." We are facing the disintegration of modern civilization. "Earth is heading towards the tipping point like a bullet train that cannot stop."

According to Jeung San Do, when this Cosmic Autumn comes, the calendar will also change and we will have 360 days in a year. This was first predicted by Confucius in the *I-Ching*, "In the future there will be 360 days in a year." Right now we have 365 days in a year and it is this 5 degrees that is causing the imbalance. When the Autumn comes, February will become the beginning of the year. As we enter the time of the Cosmic Autumn, this degree of imbalance will fall off and we will live in an age of balanced yin and yang. When this change takes place, the new principal, the new order, and the new way of balanced yin and yang will come about. But in order for that to happen, it is necessary to drop 5 degrees; this transition will bring about great catastrophes, such as earthquakes and tsunamis.

Through the story of the cosmic year we can gain an answer to what kind of time we're living in and the meaning of our lives today.

When the rule of the present calendar system changes and the Early Heaven transforms into the Later Heaven, a great shock wave will occur. The final stage of change will happen as a result of a big burst of destructive energy, of bitterness and grief caused by a vengeful history.

The shift in degrees will also bring an autumnal frost. The autumn time is a period of harvest; it is a time to gather the fruits. Just as with the autumn frost the trees bear fruit, with the cosmic autumn frost, humanity will come into fruition. The frost is the mysterious disease that is coming. According to the teachings of Eastern Learning from 160 years ago, first smallpox will recur and then a mysterious disease will sweep the world. This mysterious disease will erupt first in Korea and will invade the world for 3 years.

There is a very famous monk known as Great Master Kitano at Zentsuji Buddhist temple in Japan, and according to him, when this time of change happens, about 200 thousand people in Japan will survive, and about 4 million people in Korea will survive. If that is true, that means 99% of the Japanese will not survive. I do not want to believe that. However, the principle is that in spring time nature gives birth and in autumn nature takes away life. With the Cosmic Autumn, or *Gaebyeok*, catastrophic changes will occur. At that time our daily lives will be upset. This idea also fits with the predictions of Eastern and Western scholars as you can see below.

Predictions by Western Scholars and Futurists

The current crisis, therefore, is not just a crisis of individuals, governments, or social institutions; it is a transition of planetary dimensions... As individuals, as a society, as a civilization, and as a planetary ecosystem, we are reaching the turning point.

(*The Turning Point: Science, society, and the rising culture,* by Fritjof Capra)

"Our society is becoming so complex and interconnected that the collapse is almost inevitable." "The infrastructure required to maintain a post-industrial lifestyle-power, water, food, communication, transportation, health care, defense, finance-are all so tightly intertwined that when one system sneezes, the others can get pneumonia."

(*X Events*, by John Casti)

"The great awakening is about shifting into a mature cosmology in which we are not miserable earthworms in search of redemption, nor have we been cruelly abandoned by a distant (or absent) God. Instead, we are divine and creative beings in human form."

(*The Mystery of 2012: Predictions, Prophecies, and Possibilities*, by Gregg Braden et al.)

"This is an emergency and for emergency situations we need emergency action."

(2007. 11. Ban Ki-moon, Secretary General of UN about Global Warming)

"No challenge poses a greater threat to our future and future generations than a challenge in climate." "This is one of those rare issues, because of its magnitude, because of its scope, that if we don't get it right, we may not be able to reverse."

(President Obama, Aug. 3. 2015)

"Global warming may seem gradual in the context of a single lifetime, but in the context of the Earth's history, it is actually happening with lightning speed. Our climate crisis has become a true planetary emergency."

(*An Inconvenient Truth*, by Al Gore)

"At the surface of the ultimate "Big One", we are riding this wave together... The ultimate wave, the "Big One", is an inevitable, cyclical event within the natural evolutionary scheme."

(*Beyond Prophecies and Predictions*, by Moira Timms)

How to Overcome Gaebyeok

In order to open up the Cosmic Autumn to civilization, a new culture of spirituality must come forth to awaken all of humanity fundamentally. To accomplish this enlightenment, the spiritual culture of the Taeeulju Mantra was bestowed upon humanity by the Heavenly Father. At this time of crisis, the thing that will prevent us from this mystery disease of cosmic autumn frost is the Taeeulju Mantra. Sangjenim said, "I affixed all energy of medicine into Taeeulju Mantra." So the Taeeulju Mantra is the medicine of life that will help us awaken at this time of change from Cosmic Summer to Cosmic Autumn.

There is a book titled *Donguibogam*, which is a well-known book of medicine from the Joseon dynasty of Korea. It was registered as a World Record Heritage by Unesco, a United Nations organization. If you read this book, it says if there is an outbreak of smallpox, there is a line where it states, "No existing medicine can cure smallpox. But pray to Taeul-Gugo-Cheonjon. Sing his name."

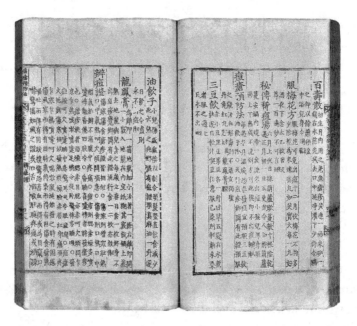

The greatest work on medicine in the history of East Asia, Dong-ui-bo-gam

The Taeeulju Mantra is the means of surviving all catastrophic changes of *Gaebyeok*. At this time, our survival is dependent upon us returning to our roots. Just as in Autumn, the plants and trees all return their energy to their roots. So also, in this time all humans must learn to receive the energy of our roots in order to survive. By becoming one with our ancestors, we can receive the energy of Autumn's fruition. We must live with appreciation and gratitude for our roots of life: Heaven, Earth and our ancestors. The Taeeulju Mantra helps us discover our roots and resolve the bitterness and grief of our ancestors. The Taeeulju Mantra brings serenity to the mind, the heavenly soul, and the earthly soul, allowing communication with the holy spirit realm. It is the mantra that will save the world's people.

We must also abandon the ways of mutual conflict, such as jealousy and slander. Instead, we must strive to make others better and help the needy and the suffering. A human being must possess the compassionate mind of mutual life-giving. The great Dao

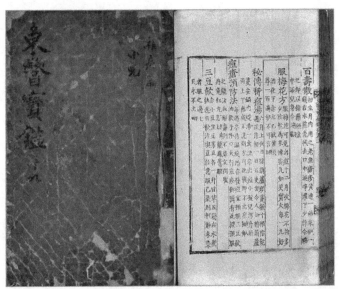

Prescription for smallpox written in Donguibogam : If you chant "Taeeul heavenly majesty who delivers all lives from suffering" a hundred times, you will experience its indescribable healing power.

of Sangjenim's boundlessness will become the way of life for all humanity in the future.

Only one who has a 50,000 year fortune may chant the Taeeulju Mantra. At the same time, all human beings can be saved by the Taeeulju Mantra. In fact, since Taeeulju is the fountain of life from Mother the Heaven, no one can survive without the Taeeulju Mantra. The energy of all medicine is also in Taeeulju. The Taeeulju Mantra overcomes all hindrances. It vanquishes all illnesses. It fulfills all wishes. It spreads the Dao of *Sangjenim* throughout the world. It delivers all humanity. It actualizes all that is willed. It is boundless and eternal. The Taeeulju Mantra is the wish-fulfilling mantra. Taesang Jondosanim has said, "The Taeeulju Mantra is the foremost life source of the present-day humanity."

Chapter 5 | Awakening the Three Elixir Fields of Life Through the Reverse Method

After passing through the three gates of enlightenment, one thing should be very clear: Meditation on the Taeeulju Mantra is the culmination of 6,000 years of ancient wisdom from the East and is the greatest necessity of our time. It is fitting, then, to close by sharing more about exactly how meditation helps us and by providing a few guidelines for the practitioner. We have already shared many of the benefits of meditation. But it is not enough just to meditate from time to time. This will not bring about the change that our world needs at this moment. We must learn to meditate throughout life, without stopping. To develop the desire for this kind of mediation, it may be required that I share a bit more about the benefits of the practice.

The first reason it is important to meditate is something I have already touched upon, which is related to the question about the meaning of life. What is the purpose of life? If we hope to understand the answer to this question, we must meditate. It offers us a period of time during which we connect with our own deepest essence. It is only through doing this that we come to experience our true purpose. When all of our activities are absorbed in the external world, we do not have access to this inner wisdom within us all. Another way we might approach this point is to say that the purpose of our existence is that we are meant to attain ultimate enlightenment. And that is possible only through meditation. The two things are intimately connected. We are born and exist for the purpose of spiritual maturation and this is achieved through meditation.

The second reason we must meditate is also a reason that I have spoken of previously. Humanity is living at the time of *gaebyeok*, which means the great opening of Heaven and Earth. This is a season of great changes. In this age, meditation is not a choice, but is a question of our survival. During the time of great change, we must practice meditation in order to survive.

The third reason we must meditate is one that I have not yet shared enough about. It is through meditation that we gain everlasting life. In daily life we waste our essence. We consume our essence; we slowly use up our life force. That is the natural path, the way of nature in this life. But at the same time, that is a path that leads to death. This wisdom can be a powerful focal point for understanding the basic mechanics of what happens in meditation. We meditate to overcome the physical death and gain everlasting spiritual life. This has been examined in detail by great enlightened ones of the East, so let me explain how this happens in more detail.

How Meditation Awakens the Three Elixir Fields of Life

There is a phrase from the teaching of Jeung San Do, that explains

The three elixir fields of Nature, Life, and Essence

how meditation helps us overcome death. "When one devotedly cultivates and purifies themselves with dao, their essence and soul become densely concentrated, so upon their death, their soul ascends to heaven and never disperses. However, when one does not cultivate and purify themselves with dao, their soul eventually dissipates into nothingness like mere smoke." (English Dojeon 9:33:1~2) In other words, after we leave the physical body on Earth and we die, there might be a second death, a death of spirit. When our spirit dies, we dissipate without leaving a trace.

Someone may ask, what kind of change occurs in your physical body that allows you to become immortal when you meditate and attain enlightenment? To answer that question, I'd like to share with you a secret about the human body. There are three forces in our body. In the spiritual cultures of the East, the creative and all-powerful force in the universe is revered as the *Samsin*, the Triune Spirit. These three are the spirit to create, the spirit to nurture and edify, and the spirit to govern. This is true for both the human body and the entire universe. God manifests in three: as creativity, as nurturing, and as governing.

Each and every person is perfectly endowed with these three sacred

The reverse method of water rising and fire descending

qualities of the Triune Spirit at the time of birth. The fundamental principles of meditation are most intimately related to these qualities. They come to be situated in three different energy centers in the body and are collectively referred to as *the three elixir fields of life*. These are related to the seven chakras, but are a simplified understanding of them. The lower energy center is in the abdomen, the middle one is the heart, and the upper one is in the head.

At birth, the spirit of creation, edification and governace of the Triune Spirit settle in our body as the Three Truths, which is nature, life and essence, the divine treasure of the Triune Spirit. The first of the three sacred elixir fields, the spirit of creation, comes to rest in the center of the brain. This spirit of creation is a light of purity and blinding brightness that transforms into human nature. This nature refers to humanity's original state of mind. The second of the three sacred elixir fields is the spirit of edification. This comes to rest in the center of the upper body, near the heart, and it transforms into human life. This second elixir field is also understood as the mandate of Heaven. The third and last of the elixir fields is the spirit of governance, and it comes to rest in the abdominal area under the navel. This transforms into human essence. It is the source of energy that governs the state of health, in both mind and body. This third and last quality is also understood as the focal point from which the road to enlightenment is paved through meditation.

Meditation is the Reverse Method

The main principle of meditation is called the Reverse Method. This is at the heart of all meditative techniques and is the secret to success. We consume and exhaust our vital energy from the day we are born to the day we die. This is the natural cycle of life for the body, but it is also the cycle that leads to death. In normal life, our essence goes down and out through our actions, our digestive system, and our sexual life. But in meditation, our essence goes in reverse. In other words, we strengthen our life and awaken our spirit. We receive life in meditation.

Through the reverse method, we awaken the three elixir fields in the body. We rouse the inert spiritual qualities slumbering in the body. We accomplish this by strengthening our essence, which is the water energy within the kidney. As the water energy rises, it goes through our spine and awakens our chakras. First it awakens our heart chakra and makes us open to our heavenly mandate that we received in our hearts. Ultimately it awakens our nature in the head chakra, which we originally received from heaven. So when we open it, we get a direct channel to Heaven.

Without meditation, the energy of fire rises to the head, not water. During daytime we do things with passion and so the fire energy from the heart rises and goes to the head. This results in stress which becomes the basis of a host of diseases including high blood pressure and diabetics.

With the reverse method, we make the water energy rise and the fire energy go down. The water goes up your spine and the fire energy comes down through your front. In meditation this reversal takes place. When the crown chakra opens, the energy of heaven comes in. Even if the crown chakra is not yet open, when you sit down to mediate this reversing process is taking place. Furthermore, when the process occurs in a more continuous way the chakras open up. When this occurs it is very intense and you will feel a burning sensation in the back of your spine. Then the three elixir fields, the heavenly essence, become awakened in the body in the form of edification, creation- transformation and governance. The essence of creation-transformation dwells in the crown chakra, edification in the heart chakra, and governance in the lower chakra.

Therefore, when we meditate it is important that we do not waste our essence. Through the nurturing of our essence, we strengthen life and awaken the spirit. What is the essence that I speak of? The word 'essence' in Korean is really the same word as sperm in English. The same word is used because the sexual energy of men and women is the essence of human energy. This is what we nurture when we meditate. People in general tend to treat their energy very lightly, and think that they can waste this essence. But this is the foundation, not only of who we are, but also of the universe. This is a very serious problem in society today. I believe it is what is wrong with capitalism. We need to understand that the energy of humans and the energy of the universe needs to be nurtured and strengthened, not wasted.

Meditation is the way to strengthen your essence. In the East, where characters are used, the word for meditation is *suhaeng*. *Su* means "to cultivate" and *haeng* means "to practice, take action, or do something." So meditation means to cultivate the movement of the body and mind. It is a way to recover your original and true spirit-- your essential nature--and transcend the death of the physical body to become an immortal spiritual being.

In English, the root of the word 'meditation' ('medi') has three meanings. The first is "to measure," the second is "to contemplate," and the third is "to heal." This is why one Indian guru said, "Meditation is the ultimate medicine." So meditation is what consolidates the essence of life. It is a beautiful and holy act that opens the doors to your true, original mind.

The Reverse Method is akin to turning the cycle of life and death on its head. This is accomplished by reversing gravity, by defying

Different methods for mantra chanting;
Quiet sitting meditation
Inner chanting
Quiet Chanting
Chanting out loud
Dynamic Meditation

the law that what goes up must come down, by moving against the tide of death. We reverse time and go backwards to our origin, to our state of being inside the womb. We go back to the origin of our consciousness, this state of being one.

The Reverse Method is the means by which the sages and those who attained enlightenment came to know the meaning of life. This method is actually a secret that isn't to be revealed. Even when someone donates billions and billions of dollars, only a small amount of this method is supposed to be transmitted. But still, I feel compelled to share it with you.

Different Kinds of Meditation

There are two basic forms of meditation, still and dynamic. In still meditation, you practice cutting off distracting thoughts while sitting in an upright posture. In this form of meditation there are three different ways to chant. The first is silently, inside the inner mind. The second is quiet chanting, in a low whispering voice. The third is chanting in a loud, clear voice.

The proper way to chant a mantra is actually to chant it out loud. So if at all possible, chant out loud. Because what is chanting?

Heo-Joon and his book on medicine, the Dong-ui-bo-gam

Chanting is the song of God; It is an expression of our divinity. The first two forms of chanting are appropriate late at night or in crowded areas, such as hotel lobbies, or airport lounges. When you are working, or you are in a place where there are a lot of people around, you can do silent meditation. If you happen to be in a busy subway, for example, you can chant in your mind or you can do very quiet chanting.

The other form of meditation is dynamic meditation. In dynamic meditation you chant a mantra in a quick tempo and your body moves in tandem with the pulse of surrounding nature. You chant mantras while standing, walking, and working. You move as if dancing and sing the song of Heaven and Earth. That is dynamic meditation. At the beginning of this chapter, I gave three reasons for doing meditation: it reveals us the meaning of life, it is critical for survival in this time of great transformation, this time of *gaebyeok*, and it reverses our energy bringing us to eternal life. For each of these same reasons, dynamic meditation is the most powerful form of meditation in this age.

The Benefits of Dynamic Meditation

We meditate to find the meaning of life. Generally, when one meditates, one sits still. This is true while practicing either the Zen method of breathing or the chanting of mantras. However, in times of crisis, due to natural disasters, or major and unforeseeable accidents, nobody can just close their eyes comfortably and practice meditation. Obviously, in those situations it would be great if we had the ability to sit still, but in such a critical situation it's not possible. Even in situations that are not as critical, it is not easy to sit still and meditate. In such situations, it may be easier to practice dynamic meditation. Furthermore, one of the reasons that meditators give up is because they have too many worldly thoughts or idle thoughts during their meditation practice. This can be easily resolved with dynamic meditation.

An even more fundamental reason to practice dynamic meditation, though, has to do with the way meditation helps us to achieve the eternal spiritual life that transcends the death of the physical body. According to traditional Eastern medicine, inside your body, there is phlegm. The phlegm I'm speaking of is different from the phlegm you spit. It flows along with the energy in your body. When you undergo excessive amounts of stress, it results in the production of excessive amounts of phlegm, the creation of dense concentrations of phlegm, or the abnormal increase of phlegm. Also, the changes in the natural environment such as rain, wind, heat, cold, thunder, lightning, and snow also produce changes in our body (cold, heat, dampness, dryness, and fever).

The *Donguibogam*, the book of Korean traditional medicine, breaks down phlegm into seventeen different varieties. The wrong kinds of phlegm are understood to be the root cause of all illness. Aging, numbness of the arms, amnesia, senility, sleeping disorders, and fatigue are all caused by phlegm. Ultimately, it is said that humans die because phlegm causes the blockage of *chi* and blood circulation.

Consistent meditation in daily life eliminates all the pathogenic phlegm in our body. When we meditate often, we will have clear-colored phlegm. As a result of this, we sleep well and make good decisions. Negative thoughts vanish, the energy of depression and sadness will dissipate, our insights will deepen, and we will become energetic and cured of the previous illnesses that have caused our body to suffer. This is the power of self-healing that happens when we get rid of phlegm through meditation.

When we do dynamic meditation, phlegm comes out of our body. What is happening is that our body is striving to be alive and is therefore excreting phlegm. If we do dynamic meditation thirty minutes, or an hour, or even three hours, it's a good idea to have a handkerchief so when we excrete phlegm we can spit it out. There are even instances reported of coughing up a whole cup of phlegm.

If no phlegm comes up in dynamic meditation, it does not mean phlegm was not excreted. It could have been excreted through

different channels. Or it could simply mean phlegm was balanced in the body through meditation.

In dynamic meditation, we can chant mantras while moving our body in search of self-healing and in total freedom. When we do this, the negative energy that has been accumulated in the mind and body from fatigue, from the pent up pressures in our internal organs, and from sadness and trauma can be erased. In this process, we receive *qi* from Heaven, and the spirit inside our body is unlocked.

When we practice dynamic meditation for even 30 minutes, it can help us relieve fatigue, release stress, and energize the body. When practiced on a daily basis over time, it will heal mental distress such as insomnia, schizophrenia, and depression.

The ultimate reason that dynamic meditation is more powerful than still meditation is that now is the time of great transformation when the cosmic seasons change. The energy of the universe goes through the reversing method at the time of change from Cosmic Summer to Cosmic Autumn. Thus, humanity must undergo the reversing method through meditation. Now is the time when enlightenment and self-healing cannot be achieved through still meditation alone. From now on, a Copernican change in the culture of meditation is required.

Instructions on Meditation Practice

Let me close by offering you some guidance for your own meditation practice. I recommend that you begin with still meditation, silent chanting, then proceed to quiet chanting, and then go on to chanting out-loud. You can switch to dynamic meditation when you get tired or restless. I will give recommendations for each of these stages. There also is a ritual to perform before engaging in meditation. It is the ritual of offering pure water and deep bows. Since we have lost the original culture, we have also lost this practice. To learn this ritual, however, you can visit a Jeung San Do Dao Center and speak with the dharma teachers.

Posture

In still meditation, proper posture is very important, specifically the way you hold your back: it must be straight. If your back is not straight, you cannot have a straight mind for your meditation. So make sure your back is straight. The importance of this right proper posture is related to the mindset all seekers should have. It is an expression of determined consciousness. Right posture is an expression of your determination to express yourself properly and righteously as who you are. It is said that the mantra is a heavenly cord that has been revealed to us to connect us to our life, our awakening, and our enlightenment. Therefore, when we chant our mantra, it is important to take the right posture to receive the mantra.

To get in the right posture for meditation, the first thing to do is straighten your back with your rear end pulled back slightly. Rock your legs from side to side two or three times and straighten your spine. Tuck your chin down slightly. You may even want to loosen your belt. When your back is straight, then you may gently, close your eyes so you don't fall into an abyss of worldly thoughts, but at the same time you are able to stay in an awakened state.

Crowd of people chanting the mantras

Breath

When we want to understand how to chant, we first have to understand breath. Obviously, your breath is integrally important to life. If your breath stops, your body dies. To breathe properly for meditation, start with an empty mind, a comfortable mind. Now with your eyes closed softly begin to breathe deeply and naturally. Comfortably forgetting all worldly thoughts. Breathe in with an encompassing mind. Breathe out naturally and comfortably. Breathe in with a loving mind, a pleasant mind. Breathe in with a quiet mind. Breathe in with a thoughtful mind for all existence, for our parents, for our ancestral beings.

Breathe in with the thought of consciously pulling your inner chi from the center of yin energy. When you breathe out, feel your energy descend from the top of the head, which is the center of yang energy, to the lower energy centers. This breathing method is for silent chanting but you ignore this when chanting mantras out loud.

Pictures of the 2016 Taeeulju concert event at Times Center, New York City.

Chanting

When chanting begins by trying to silently chant the Taeeulju Mantra within your mind. Straighten your back, and chant to the rhythm of your respiration. Slowly inhale and exhale as you chant within your mind. Next chant softly so that only you can hear your own voice. Continue breathing in the same way. Next, try chanting out loud. In order to accept the effects of the mantra's sound and receive the mantra's divine energy, you must completely empty your mind and chant with a clear voice.

When you chant the mantra, make sure you still have strong posture and then abandon all thoughts, all language, and all logic. Abandon whatever you think you are and whatever you think about the universe. Make sure to have an empty mind and with the empty mind receive the language of the universe, the divine language of the mantra. Abandon knowledge and logic. Abandon whatever power you think you have in the world. Just abandon it all. When you do this, then you can receive the divinity of the mantra. We need to be like the innocent children. We need to abandon our worldly thoughts. Until we do this, we cannot really understand the world of the mantra.

The Taeeulju Mantra is related to the other 9 mantras that Jeungsan Sangjenim gave us. These ten mantras contain the mystery of life and the world but the Taeeulju Mantra is the most important of these. When you adopt this mantra, it is best if you determine your mind to pursue meditation for at least 10 years. With that determination you can pursue meditation properly.

Dynamic Meditation

If you begin to have lots of worldly thoughts when sitting in still meditation, that's when you can switch to dynamic meditation. You can also change to dynamic meditation when your leg feels numb during still meditation. You may even begin when you are very tired, you can center your meditation on the dynamic method.

Dynamic meditation is any kind of movement that you make while you chant the mantra, whether that means stretching or simply moving your hands or feet. When you do still meditation, your legs may fall asleep, or you may start to come up with many different thoughts. So you might begin your meditation by doing still meditation and then change into dynamic meditation naturally if this happens. Dynamic meditation is based on sitting meditation, but it reverses the method of quiet sitting meditation.

Mentality

When you recite mantra, it is very important not to chant in a sorrowful voice, even if you feel depressed or you happen to be in a state of suffering. One day, a doctor came to me and said his younger brother got into an accident and broke his ankle, even though he was chanting this mantra. So the doctor asked me why that happened to his brother? So I asked him, "When he chants his mantra, does he chant his mantra in a depressed tone or in a crying voice?" And. in fact, he was chanting that way.

I told the doctor that if he chants in a crying voice, Heaven will answer by giving him an occasion to cry. This idea is simple, but fundamental. So even if you are suffering due to hardships or tribulations, you must not chant with a sad voice. If you chant with a sad voice, you will undergo misfortune because Heaven and Earth's negative energy will reciprocate with the gloomy sound of mantra chanting. So please do it with happiness and joyfulness!

Conclusion

We are witnessing the arrival of a new era during which we will see the popularization of enlightenment. It is the era of the Supreme Dao of Mugeuk, of infinite wisdom. This will fully activate the divinity within our bodies. This is the essence of the Eastern Learning. The term *Eastern* in Eastern Learning does not just refer to the direction. It also means the place where the principles of nature and civilization are reborn. The term *Learning* has two meanings, *Dao* and *Gyo*. *Dao* means the *way* of the ultimate level of enlightenment. *Gyo* is the teaching of a universal lifestyle of humanity beyond religions. So when we say this is the Supreme Dao of Mugeuk, we mean that this is the path that unites Heaven, Earth, and humanity into one. This is the Dao that builds the new order of civilization.

The message of Jeung San Do is that we must usher in a new era of universal culture and overcome the limitations of the civilizations of the East and West. To accomplish this, we must resolve the problems that humanity faces today at their very root. This resolution must occur during this time of *gaebyeok,* this transition time from the Cosmic Summer (and the order of mutual conflict), to the Cosmic Autumn and Winter, to the time of the order of mutual life-bettering and life-saving.

The way to accomplish this is to meditate with one mind, to return to our original mind. We must purify our body every morning with the Taeeulju Mantra. The Taeeulju Mantra is the holiest mantra. With this mantra anyone can become a Buddha, attain enlightenment, and become completely healed. This mantra is our first and foremost life source. We must chant it as if we are breathing oxygen. Empty your mind and chant the Taeeulju Mantra. You will be able to feel the utmost holiness and the utmost enlightenment. Anyone can experience this.

Learning One Mind
The Three Gates of Enlightenment
9 week workshops:

Awakening to the Original Spiritual Culture of
Humanity

CONTENTS

Learning One Mind
The Three Gates of Enlightenment
9 week workshops:

Awakening to the Original Spiritual Culture of
Humanity

Week One
What is the Mind?

❁ The center of heaven and earth is the mind.
Therefore, heaven and earth's east, west, south, and north
and the human body
all depend upon the mind.
(Dojeon 2:105:2)

❁ If heaven provides meager rain and dew,
woes inevitably arise in all lands.
If earth employs meager water and soil in nurturing all life,
woes inevitably arise in all life.
If people are meager in their spreading of virtue,
woes inevitably arise in all affairs.

The provision of rain and dew by heaven,
the employment of water and soil by earth,
the spreading of virtue by people
—these all depend upon the mind.
The mind is the hinge, the gate, and the pathway of the spirits.
The spirits open and close the hinge,
enter and leave through the gate,
and come and go along the pathway.
Sometimes spirits are benevolent, sometimes malevolent.
If you emulate what is good, and if you reform what is wicked,
your mind—the hinge, the gate, the pathway—
will indeed be a fount of creation-transformation greater than
heaven and earth.
(Dojeon 4:75:5-7)

The human mind is the master of all spirits in heaven and earth.

The human body is the house of yin and yang's creation-transformation.

Enlightenment is attained through one's own dao of creation-transformation.

Do not think of being benevolent,

Do not think of being malevolent.

By forgetting my form, forgetting my existence,
my flesh no longer exists, I do not exist—nothing exists.

I then penetrate the heavenly realm above
and pierce the depths of the earth below.

(by Ahn Un-san, His Holiness the Taesang Jongdosanim)

Week Two
What is Time?

❀ I wield the fourfold principle of birth, growth, harvest, and rest—
   this is the way of change through non-action. (Dojeon 2:16:1)
❀ If heaven deviates from its principle, nothing can exist.
   (Dojeon 2:16:3)
❀ The way of heaven and earth is origination, proliferation, benefit,
   and firmness .... (Dojeon 10:75:3)

❀ Water, fire, metal, and wood wax and peak,
      having awaited their proper time.
   Water arises from fire,
      thus, there is no absolute mutual conflict and domination under
      heaven.
   (Dojeon 4:103:3)

❀ Release, dispersion, spirit, and dao—
      this is the grand order and law of change.
   The *qi* of spring is release.
   The *qi* of summer is dispersion.
   The *qi* of autumn is spirit.
   The *qi* of winter is dao.
   I govern the grand order of heaven and earth's four seasons
      through *qi*.
   (Dojeon 6:85:8)

❀ The sun and moon rule all existence without prejudice.
      Rivers and mountains embrace all actions with dao.
   (Dojeon 5:92:5)

❀ All of heaven and earth's principles lie within change (역 易).
   (Dojeon 2:16:5)

Week Three
What is God?

❁ Now is the age of heaven and earth's achievement of their
purpose. The Autumn God embraces the mandate of governing
all beings to gather all enlightened knowledge for the greatest of
all fulfillments—such is *gaebyeok*.

When the autumn wind blows, some come to fruition while
others wither and fall. The true will bear glorious fruit and gain
life everlasting; the false will wither and fall, suffering death
eternal. So it is that the spirits of heaven and earth will wield their
authority to purge unrighteousness, but the spirits will serve the
righteous with benevolence and love. And so, you who seek life
and blessings must ardently strive to be righteous. (Dojeon 4:21)

❁ Matteo Ricci contributed vast meritorious deeds and virtue to
the world. In this age of the resolution of bitterness and grief,
he presides as the head spirit of the spirit realm. All who know
this should never speak of him save with reverence. Yet, people
remain unaware of Matteo Ricci's meritorious deeds and virtue
because he benefited the world inconspicuously.
Matteo Ricci, a Westerner, came to the East and offered many
ways to build the kingdom of heaven on earth, but his vision
never came to pass, because he could not correct all the corrupt
practices that had become entrenched over the ages. Yet, he did
succeed in casting down the boundaries between the East and
West, enabling the spirits, who guarded the borders and could not
travel to one another's regions, to cross borders unhindered.
After his death, Matteo Ricci led preeminent spirits of civilizations
in the East to the West and again sought to build the kingdom of
heaven on earth. From that time forth, the spirits inside the earth
began ascending to heaven to learn its marvelous ways and then

returning to earth to breathe inspiration into people. It is this that fostered the advancement of scholarship and the development of sophisticated machines, enabling humanity to model its civilization after that of the kingdom of heaven and hence raise up modern civilization. The material conveniences of Western civilization were modeled upon heaven's civilization.

This new civilization, however, became enlightened about only the material world and its principles, and so it cultivated arrogance and brutality and sought to conquer nature with power mighty enough to shake both heaven and earth, unhesitatingly committing every form of wickedness.

Thus, the authority of the way of the spirits collapsed, and the three realms fell into terrible disorder, causing both the way of heaven and human affairs to contravene the dosu of heaven and earth.

In response, Matteo Ricci assembled all the ancient divine sages, buddhas, and bodhisattvas, then ascended to the ninth heaven and there entreated me to address the catastrophic plight of humans and spirits.

In answer to their plea, I descended to the canopy tower in the Nation of Great Law in the West, and after traveling the world while surveying the three realms, attended by Matteo Ricci, I came to this Eastern land, Joseon. (Dojeon 2:26:1-12)

❀ I am Maitreya. The Maitreya statue at Geumsansa Temple holds a wish-fulfilling jewel in its hand, but I hold one in My mouth. (Dojeon 10:23:5)

❀ Those who believe in Jesus await the second coming of Jesus, those who believe in Buddha await the coming of Maitreya Buddha, and those who believe in Eastern Learning await the rebirth of Choe Su-un. But whoever this person proves to be, when that one person comes, all will proclaim him their master and follow him. (Dojeon 2:36:1-4)

Week Four
What is Meditation?

❀ People speak with one another yet never actually fathom each other's minds. People do not know one another's minds, so it is indeed most difficult to attain harmony. (Dojeon 11:87:1-2)

❀ Enlightenment into the principles of the stars in heaven requires the mastery of yin and yang's cycle throughout the four seasons. Enlightenment into the principles of earth requires the mastery of harvesting a myriad bountiful crops. Enlightenment into humanity's right path requires the mastery of how all existence arises and evolves. (Dojeon 11:87:3-5)

❀ When one devotedly cultivates and purifies themselves with dao, their essence and soul become densely concentrated, so upon their death, their soul ascends to heaven and never disperses. However, when one does not cultivate and purify themselves with dao, their soul eventually dissipates into nothingness like mere smoke. (Dojeon 9:33:1-2)

The expression *one mind of heaven and earth* has two meanings. The first is that heaven and earth are walking only one path: birth, growth, harvest, and rest. This is the dao of heaven and earth. When we awaken to this path, it is not a simple understanding, but a deep sensitivity and awareness of nature. The second meaning is that, as a child of heaven and earth, I become one with my parents. This is to become one with the great parents, the source of life, heaven and earth. In the state of one mind, heaven and earth eternally walk down the path of creativity. They are yin and yang in balance, a perfect state of harmony.

Week Five
What is Life?

❀ Origination, proliferation, benefit, and firmness
   arise from the cycle of the sun and moon.
The sun and moon illuminate humanity's viscera and entrails,
   enabling a brilliant attainment of resplendent virtue.
(Dojeon 2:113:2)

❀ It is for humanity that heaven and earth came into being;
It is for humanity that the sun and moon circulate and illuminate;
It is for humanity that yin and yang wax and wane;
It is for humanity that the order of the four seasons observes harmony;
It is for humanity that all existence comes into being;
It is to edify and to save humanity that sages are born.
Since heaven and earth cannot attain fruition without humanity,
   heaven and earth beget, in balance, humanity and all existence.
(Dojeon 11:98:4-10)

❀ One day, Sangjenim recited the following to his disciples:

事之當旺 在於天地 必不在於人
然 無人 無天地故 天地生人 用人
以人生 不參於天地用人之時 何可曰人生乎

The prosperity of a work depends upon heaven and earth, not
necessarily upon humans. Yet, in the absence of humans, it is as
though heaven and earth do not exist. Hence, heaven and earth
beget humans and consummate their purpose through them. You
have been born as a human being in this era when heaven and
earth consummate their purpose through humans, so how can
you be considered a human if you do not take part? (Dojeon 8:69)

Week Six
What is History?

❃ The Early Heaven is ruled by the destiny of mutual conflict and domination. The principle of mutual conflict and domination has governed all humanity and all existence, and so heaven and earth have never known a single moment free of war. Therefore, bitterness and grief now fills all the world. As the destiny of mutual conflict and domination is about to be brought to an end, colossal catastrophes threaten to erupt all at once, annihilating the human world. (Dojeon 2:13:1-4)

❃ Since ancient times, all wars and feuds among the tribes of different lands have arisen from a lack of unification between regional spirits and terrestrial *qi*. Therefore, unification between regional spirits and terrestrial *qi* will be the fundamental impetus for peace among humanity.
All tribes had unique experiences that led to particular ways of thinking and hence to the formation of distinct cultures, which inevitably provoked disputes when one culture encountered another. Thus, I now extract and gather the essence of each culture to lay the foundation of the Later Heaven's civilization. (Dojeon 4:18)

❃ I will now ascend Hoemunsan Mountain to establish a new order for heaven and earth. I will destine the grand tides of the world through the spiritual *qi* of an auspicious site known as Five Immortals Playing Baduk, where two immortals contest a match, two offer advice, and one is the master of the game. The master, unable to take sides, observes the match and devotes himself solely to accommodating the guests. Since the wherewithal of his household is not particularly lacking, the master fulfills his duties as long as he does not neglect propriety in accommodating the guests. When the match reaches its conclusion and everyone else departs, the game board and the stones return to the master. Han Gaozu long ago gained the world on horseback, but we will gain the world while seated. (Dojeon 5:5)

Week Seven
What is Healing?

✦ After conferring upon Subunim the dominion of the Subu, Sangjenim proclaimed, "I am the Autumn God. It is the Autumn God who wields supreme authority, yet even the Autumn God cannot act at will if the Subu disapproves."

From that time forth, when Sangjenim was making decisions during various works of renewal, He made certain to consult Subunim about every decision and only thereafter completed the work of renewal. He declared, "All who stray from the shadow of the Subu's skirt shall die." (Dojeon 6:25)

✦ The Early Heaven is the world of oppressed yin and revered yang. The bitterness and grief of women fills heaven and earth, impeding the course of heaven and earth's destiny; consequently, colossal catastrophes threaten to burst forth and ultimately destroy the human world. Therefore, if the bitterness and grief of women is not resolved, even the emergence of a preeminent person possessing both a divine nature and scholarly and military excellence will not suffice to deliver the world.

Though yin has been oppressed and yang revered, the expression is 'yin and yang,' and so people always say 'yin' before 'yang.' This is indeed peculiar. From this time forth, everything will be reformed in accordance with this saying. (Dojeon 2:44)

✦ Sangjenim proclaimed, "Now is the age of the resolution of bitterness and grief. Deeply and completely trapped for thousands of years, women have been treated as no more than servants and objects of men's pleasure, but I will resolve the bitterness of women to reestablish Geon and Gon in accordance with right yin and right yang. I will recraft propriety between men and women to prevent men from exercising their rights arbitrarily without considering the counsel of women."

One day, after conducting a work of renewal, Sangjenim wrote upon a sheet of paper that He subsequently burned, "Magnificent women. Magnificent men."

(Dojeon 4:50)

❁ The clicking of women turning prayer beads in their desire to overturn the world resounds throughout the nine heavens. These women yearn for a heaven and earth dominated by women. However, this will not come to pass. I will instead usher in an age of equality between men and women. When entrusting my work to people, I will employ men and women without discrimination.

(Dojeon 2:45:1-3)

Week Eight
What is Salvation?

🌼 Now is the age of heaven and earth's achievement of their purpose. At my command, the spirits of heaven and earth will purge unrighteousness and inconspicuously aid the righteous in accordance with the righteousness that is the destiny of autumn. The evil will fall like autumn leaves and perish, while the true will ripen into the bountiful fruits of autumn. (Dojeon 2:39:4-6)

🌼 All the Early Heaven's malevolent karma and all of the spirits' bitterness, grief, and vengeance are combining to create the illness of the world, which will one day manifest as the mysterious disease. There has been no illness of such magnitude in spring and summer. When the season transitions to autumn, retribution for the sins of spring and summer will spawn the terrible disease. (Dojeon 7:30)

🌼 You hold within your hand the word *saeng* (生), which means 'to save life'—is now not the autumn, in which humans fulfill the will of heaven and earth? My work shall be accomplished through three stages of change. The work of heaven and earth rests at the divide between life and death, and our ceaseless struggle is the work of earning three meals a day. Our work is to survive when others die and to flourish with glory and prosperity when others merely survive. (Dojeon 8:83)

Week Nine
What is Enlightenment?

🌼 Heaven and earth would be empty shells
  without the sun and moon.
 The sun and moon would be empty shadows
  without people possessing supreme devotion. (Dojeon 6:8:4)

🌼 文明開化三千國 道術運通九萬里

 The new civilization of autumn blooms into three thousand
 nations.
 The grand destiny of the dao mastery civilization ripples to the
 ends of the universe. (Dojeon 5:166:5)

🌼 One day Sangjenim wrote out the verses of the Taeeulju Mantra
 as follows:

吽哆
吽哆　太乙天 上元君 吽哩哆哪都來 吽哩喊哩 娑婆訶

Hoom-chi

　　　Tae-eul-cheon Sang-won-gun
　　　Hoom-ri-chi-ya-do-rae Hoom-ri-ham-ri-sa-pa-ha
Hoom-chi

Having written the mantra, he asked his disciples, "What does the mantra's shape suggest to you?"

"The shape reminds me of a spoon," Gap-chil replied.

"I will intermingle the East and West like *bibimbap*," Sangjenim declared, "and you will partake of it with this spoon. The Taeeulju Mantra, shaped like a spoon, is the mark of sustenance. If this mark is posted on your houses, the spirits of the mysterious disease will recognize your homes as houses of dao and refrain from trespassing within." (Dojeon 7:56)

◈ Resist the onrush of sleep and chant the Taeeulju Mantra countless times. Taeeulcheon Sangwongun is the most sovereign emperor of heaven, and so the Taeeulju Mantra will be chanted in every village and in every school for fifty thousand years. (Dojeon 7:58:1-2)

◈ *Hoom-chi* is the sound of calling out to the parents, heaven and earth. It is the sound of humanity calling out to God like a calf lowing to its mother. (Dojeon 7:57:1-2)

◈ The Taeeulju Mantra is medicine. (Dojeon 4:101:4)

◈ Sin-nong saved many lives by tasting a hundred herbs to devise medicine, but we will save countless lives throughout the world by chanting the Taeeulju Mantra. (Dojeon 4:101:1-2)

Taeeulju Mantra Meditation Experiences in Pictures

The human mind is the master of all spirits in heaven and earth. The human body is the house of yin and yang's creation-transformation. Enlightenment is attained through one's own dao of creation-transformation.

(Ahn Un-san, His Holiness the Taesang Jongdosanim)

Concentrate on chanting mantras with a true heart.
Straighten your back. Become one with the source of the universe.
(Ahn Ahn Gyeong-jeon, His Holiness the Jongdosanim)

The Taeeulju Mantra calls out to the original ancestor (womb, origin) of all beings in heaven and earth to become one with the great sea of life in the universe. It enlightens us to the realm of spirits and heals disease. The Taeeulju Mantra has many benefits. One major benefit is healing which leads to complete health of mind, body, and spirit. Another is having peace of mind and experiencing the light of the universe which leads us to enlightenment. The Taeeulju Mantra gives us protection against accidents, disasters, or illnesses.

Hoom-chi Hoom-chi Tae-eul-cheon Sang-won-gun
Hoom-ri-chi-ya-do-rae Hoom-ri-ham-ri-sa-pa-ha

This is a picture of a regular water molecule that had not received the Healing Energy of Taeeulju Mantra.

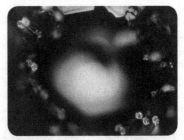

This is a picture of a water molecule that had received the Healing Energy of Taeeulju Mantra. It formed a perfect six sided water crystal.

Taeeulju Mantra Aurora pictures: The broken aurora was healed and became stronger after 2 hours of Taeeulju Mantra Meditation.

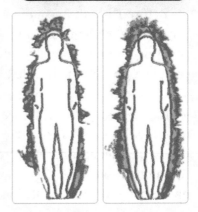

Taeeulju Mantra blood test:

After 2 hours of Taeeulju Mantra Meditation, the cholesterol in the blood disappeared and each red blood cell looks much healthier and stronger.

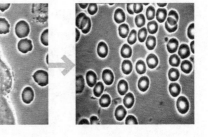

Individual Taeeulju Mantra Meditation Healing Experiences

After my serious car accident, one day I became very angry and said, "Enough already, I'm not going to take any pain killers today." That day, with much pain in my body, I went to bed and played the Taeeulju Mantra Meditation Healing tape. After a few minutes, I felt an enormous energy penetrating into my feet and into the top of my head, and then it filled my entire body. The next day I was able to walk, and what a blessing it was, not to have any pain in my body. As I continued to meditate little by little, I had returned to my normal self.

N. D.

Before I began Taeeulju Mantra meditation, I had a benign breast tumor about one inch in diameter. After three days of chanting and receiving Taeeulju Mantra Healing, my tumor had completely disappeared. It felt as if my energy was being purified and transformed. I felt a release of negative energies and an opening feeling inside my heart. I felt a strong feeling of love and warmth inside me and a sense of inner peace and tranquility. When I am receiving Taeeulju Mantra Healing energy, I experience many sensations. I sometimes feel a warm and radiant energy coming from my Taeeulju Mantra Meditation teacher and from above my head. I sometimes see rays of light and experience an emotional release of joy. Other times, I feel that my energy is being detoxified and I can feel an active removal of negative energy. I feel a strong vibration inside my body from chanting Taeeulju Mantra, especially chanting in a group. When I am feeling this vibration, I feel a sense of connection to a greater spiritual energy in the universe. I am grateful that I have been introduced to Taeeulju Mantra meditation. I feel that I have been deeply touched. I am hopeful that I will someday be able to heal others who continue to suffer from spiritual and emotional injuries.

R. L.

My mother called me one afternoon with a tone of shock and panic. She had a mammogram earlier that day and a lump in her breast was found. The doctors wanted to move quickly, scheduling appointments for various tests and treatments which would cause emotional as well as physical pain and stress. We talked for a while as the conversation evolved to the Tae-eul Mantra. Mom has been to some workshops and knew the mantra. I suggested that I go to her house so we could conduct a Taeeulju Mantra Healing Ritual. The next afternoon we conducted the ritual. My mother and I are very close, but the two of us chanting together was powerful and touching. As mother and daughter, the bonding that occurred was magical. Nothing existed but two of us, the Taeeulju Mantra energy and our spiritual help. The room was full of our love and trust for each other and what we were doing. It was an experience we will always remember. The tests were re-taken at another facility with state-of-the-art equipment. Good News! Her lump was gone!

L. T.

On March 13, 1996, a biopsy diagnosed my having prostate cancer at a level that required immediate surgery. At age 61, with a wide range of life experiences and having been a world traveler, things do not usually upset me. Yet this news unnerved me completely. After going through a period of severe depression, I failed to follow through on a series of tests to determine if the cancer had spread. I managed, with the help of my sister, to get out of the house and attend the New Age Expo. Here, I experienced a Taeeulju Mantra Meditation that aroused my curiosity and interest. I became more focused and decided, rather than do nothing, participate in the nine-week healing meditation workshops. During the period of the workshop series, I received healings and played the healing meditation tape at night while I slept. My spirits uplifted a little. They really soared when I received the results of the second biopsy that revealed there was no cancer present in any of the tissues' samples.

C. P.

It started with a burning sensation all along my spine and on the top of my head. Since I had never chanted before I had no idea what I was feeling. I began to shed my outermost layer of clothing in an effort to cool down. This, of course, did not help. At one point, the heat in the room became too intense that I quickly opened my eyes to see what was going on. For a moment, I thought that the candles in the front of the room had started a fire. By the end of the meditation, the initial discomfort I felt was replaced by a strong feeling of inner peace and joyfulness that seemed to permeate every fiber of my being. It was only after a discussion of my experience at the end of the workshop that I realized what I had been feeling was the powerful healing energy of Taeeulju Mantra. The powerful healing energy of the Taeeulju Mantra has helped me heal not only my spirit but my physical body as well. Within a month of chanting Taeeulju Mantra I was also able to dissolve a fibroid growth that I had been suffering from for many years.

C. A.

Since 1977, I have had numerous emergency room visits and hospitalizations due to cardiac problems: irregular and slow heartbeats (arrhythmia) and pauses in heart activity (sick sinus syndrome) with ever increasing episodes and longer pauses. Last December, after a 24 hour Holter Monitor Electrocardiogram, I was informed that I need a surgically implanted pacemaker. Through diligently learning and practicing Taeeulju Mantra meditations along with individual healings by the most compassionate and conscientious NY Doh-jang staff, the March 28, 1996 report indicated that no pacemaker is required at all.

The pauses were virtually eliminated, a 90% decrease (from 166 down to 17 pauses with no significant time lengths) and the arrhythmia were reduced by 81.5%

L. H.